Conducting a Survey

Techniques for a Term Project

Lawrence T. Orcher

Pyrczak Publishing
P.O. Box 250430 • Glendale, CA 91225

"Pyrczak Publishing" is an imprint of Fred Pyrczak, Publisher, A California Corporation.

Project Director: Monica Lopez.

Cover design by Robert Kibler and Larry Nichols.

Editorial assistance provided by Cheryl Alcorn, Randall R. Bruce, Brenda Koplin, Jack Petit, Erica Simmons, and Sharon Young.

Printed in the United States of America by Malloy, Inc.

ISBN 1-884585-72-8

Contents

Notes:

Detailed Contents

Notes:

Introduction

This book provides step-by-step instructions on how to conduct a survey.

The Audience for This Book

This book is designed for students who will be conducting their first survey as a term project. Unlike other texts on research methods, this text covers only methods that are realistic for use by students with limited resources and time, such as a single semester in which the survey is planned, conducted, and written up.

It is assumed that the students who will be using this book have little or no background in research methods or statistics. Hence, concrete, nontheoretical advice is given throughout.

The book is an ideal supplement for research methods courses. While main textbooks for such courses are broad in their scope, which is necessary in order to provide an overview of the entire endeavor of conducting research, this text is limited in its focus. This limited focus makes it easy for students to identify the essentials for a term project.

Students in content-area classes in the social and behavioral sciences will also benefit from this book because the book provides enough support that students can conduct surveys with little supervision by instructors, even if the students have not taken courses in research methodology.

Benefits of Conducting a Term-Project Survey

The first-hand experience of conducting a survey as a term project helps students become realistic about the nature and quality of knowledge generated by empirical research.

More specifically, it helps them understand both the contributions and limitations of survey research methods.

As students plan and conduct their surveys, they learn that all survey research methods have pitfalls, some of which are not possible to overcome. For instance, obtaining an adequate sample under many circumstances can be quite difficult. Also for many survey research topics, existing measuring instruments (e.g., questionnaires) are not available, and new ones must be constructed and used even if time does not permit independent formal studies of the reliability and validity of the new instruments.

Having had the experience of failing to conduct a "perfect" survey, students become more realistic about the limitations of knowledge provided by published surveys.

In addition, the experience of successfully conducting a term-project survey gives students the confidence to work on more elaborate surveys in the future, such as a survey for a master's degree project.

Distinctive Features

The distinctive features of this book are:

- A nontheoretical yet intellectually sound presentation of survey research methods. This keeps students from getting bogged down in issues not directly relevant to conducting a survey.

- The large number of examples throughout the book provide concrete guidance on what to do and how to do it.

- An emphasis on the use of a limited number of descriptive statistics with easy-to-compute margins of error, which keeps students from becoming overly confident in their results.

About the Appendices

Appendix A provides guidance on preparing a research proposal for a survey. If a proposal is required by the instructor, this appendix should be read as soon as possible. Note that Appendix A is coordinated with Chapter 14 (Writing a Survey Research Report), so Chapter 14 should also be read at the time a proposal is being prepared.

Appendix B provides an overview of issues in reliability and validity as they apply to instruments used to collect data in a survey. Students who use previously published instruments for which there is reliability and validity data will want to consult this appendix in order to better understand the statistical properties of the instruments they are using.

Appendix C introduces significance testing, an issue not covered in the body of this book. Students with some training in statistics may want to conduct significance tests using knowledge from statistics courses they have previously taken. This appendix will help such students review the purposes of significance testing. Note that while significance testing is not explicitly covered in the body of this text, margins of error, which are the building blocks of significance testing, are described.

Appendix D provides information on using computer programs to calculate statistics, with special attention to programs on the Internet that are both easy to use and available free of charge.

Acknowledgments

Richard Rasor of American River College provided many helpful comments on the first draft of this book.

I am especially indebted to Mildred L. Patten, who served as consulting editor. In addition to providing guidance on the entire project, she graciously allowed me to use examples from her textbook, *Questionnaire Research*: *A Practical Guide* (Pyrczak Publishing, 2001). These examples are primarily found in the last half of this book and in the appendices.

Lawrence T. Orcher

Chapter 1

A Survey As a Term Project

A *survey* is a study in which data are collected to describe the characteristics of a population. Unlike an *experiment*, in which treatments are given to influence the participants, in a survey, researchers avoid influencing participants. This is because the researchers' goal in conducting surveys is to describe respondents as they naturally exist without intervention.[1]

Overview of Steps in Conducting a Survey

Conducting a survey as a term project involves the same basic steps as a survey conducted by a professional survey research organization. However, for a term project, a survey is usually conducted in a limited timeframe with limited resources by students who have limited training in research methods and statistics. This book is designed to help students conduct satisfactory surveys despite these limitations.

Identifying Broad Problem Areas

The first step in conducting a survey is to identify a broad problem area from which a topic for a survey will be identified.

For a content-area course such as Speech Pathology (in Special Education) or Ethnicity and Race Relations (in Sociology), the broad problem area for a survey typically will be dictated by the content of the course. Skimming the course textbook as well as the instructor's syllabus usually will help in selecting a broad problem area for a survey for such a course. (See Examples 1.1 and 1.2 on the next page.)

For a research methods course, such as Methods of Research in Psychology, the scope of suitable broad problem areas typically is much wider than in a content-area course. The instructor of a methods course might allow selection of any problem area that relates to the student's major discipline.

Note that in either type of course an instructor may put delimitations on the topics for the term projects or may even assign a broad problem area (or even a narrow problem area) for all students to explore in a survey.

Ideally, a student should identify two or more potential broad problem areas and request feedback. Feedback from other students and the instructor on the suitability of the areas can assist in selecting among them. In most cases, the broad problem area will need to be narrowed in order to make the project manageable within a single semester.

---

[1] A study in which a researcher provides an intervention (i.e., treatment) is called an *experiment*. A survey is a *nonexperimental* study.

Narrowing the broad problem area that is selected as the basis for a survey is illustrated in the examples below and is discussed in more detail in Chapters 2 and 3.

Formulating Research Purposes and Hypotheses

For a term project, the research purpose for a survey should usually be rather narrow in order to keep the project focused and manageable. Examples 1.1 and 1.2 show research purposes for two types of courses.

Example 1.1

A broad problem area and a related research purpose for a course in speech communication:

Course title: Fluency Disorders

Broad problem area: Stuttering

Narrower problem area: Teachers' knowledge of stuttering

Research purpose for a survey: To determine elementary school teacher-candidates' knowledge of techniques for working with students who stutter.

Example 1.2

A broad problem area and a related research purpose for a course in sociology:

Course title: Ethnicity and Race Relations

Broad problem area: Racial/ethnic self-segregation

Narrower problem area: Self-segregation by college students

Research purpose: To identify the reasons college students cite for engaging in self-segregation in the college cafeteria.

In Example 1.1, the purpose involves measuring knowledge. In Example 1.2, the purpose involves measuring reasons respondents give for engaging in a certain type of behavior. Surveys can also be used to examine attitudes (such as attitudes toward students who stutter) and opinions (such as opinions on the adequacy of teacher preparation courses for working with students who stutter).[2]

A *research hypothesis* is a prediction of the outcome of a survey. Based on a hunch or based on the findings of previous research, a hypothesis might be formulated. Example 1.3 shows a hypothesis that is related to the research purpose in Example 1.1. Note that the term "inadequate knowledge" should be defined before conducting the research (e.g., an average score of less than 70% on a specific test).

---

[2] An *attitude* is a relatively stable general predisposition toward some entity (e.g., attitude toward the Republican party), while an *opinion* generally is more focused and potentially more transient (e.g., opinion on a particular Republican candidate for president).

Example 1.3

A research hypothesis for the research purpose in Example 1.1:

Research hypothesis: Elementary school teacher-candidates have inadequate knowledge of techniques for working with students who stutter.

Note that all surveys should have one or more specific purposes. However, it is not necessary to formulate a hypothesis before undertaking a survey. Hypotheses should be formulated only if the researcher believes he or she can predict the outcome of the survey.

Practical versus Theoretical Underpinnings

The underpinnings of the purpose for a survey may be of a purely practical, applied nature. For instance, a survey on the hours of operation of the college cafeteria might be conducted for the practical purpose of determining which hours will best suit the needs of students.

On the other hand, the underpinnings of the purpose for a survey may be of a theoretical nature. A scientific theory[3] is a unified explanation of how variables relate to each other and why they do so. A survey that contributes to the understanding of a theory makes a contribution to a broader understanding of an issue than a survey that is conducted only for practical decision-making purposes. In addition, the explanations provided by theories can serve as the underpinnings for a research hypothesis (i.e., a hypothesis that, if confirmed, would support the theory).

Issues in formulating research purposes and research hypotheses and their practical and theoretical bases are explored and illustrated in more detail in Chapter 3.

Locating Related Literature and Writing a Literature Review

On almost any broad problem area, there is a large volume of related literature, often published in academic journals. This literature should be examined at the same time that the problem area is being narrowed and the research purposes or hypotheses are being formulated because interesting ideas for a term-project survey can often be found in such literature.

In addition to getting topic ideas by surveying literature, ideas can be obtained for methods to use in conducting a survey on a particular topic. For instance, survey instruments (such as questionnaires) used in previous research can be identified for possible use in a term-project survey.

With permission of the instructor, a survey conducted as a term project might be a *replication* of a published survey described in the literature. A replication is an attempt to mimic a previous study to see if the same types of results can be obtained again. *Replicability* is an important criterion in the evaluation of research findings. Researchers put more faith in

---

[3] The term *scientific theory* is used here to refer to any theory that has been described in academic publications, such as journals, and for which there is some published research attesting to its validity.

those results that can be clearly replicated than in results that may be viewed as idiosyncratic because other researchers have difficulty independently replicating them.

For a term project, it could be interesting to conduct a *modified replication* in which the term-project survey has the same purpose and basically the same research methodology as a previously published survey but with some variations, such as using a different type of respondent or modified measuring instruments.

Techniques for surveying literature and using literature in refining the topic for a term project are described in Chapter 4. Preparing a formal literature review to include in a term-project research report is described in Chapter 5.

Preparing a Research Proposal

Preparing a full-fledged research proposal can be a term project in and of itself. In fact, some instructors may require students only to write research proposals for surveys, without actually conducting the surveys.

Most students who are using this book will be conducting surveys (not just proposing them). For these students, it is very desirable to prepare a proposal before conducting their surveys, even if the proposals are very brief and informal. Sharing the proposals with other students and the instructor for feedback can help in refining research plans and avoiding misunderstandings regarding the instructor's expectations. In addition, most of the material in a proposal can be used in the final term-project research report, making it easier to complete the project on time. Writing the final report is discussed in Chapter 14.

In addition, colleges very often require that students obtain permission before conducting research. Those who provide permission (such as a faculty committee) will almost always need to see a written proposal before granting permission.

Appendix A provides guidelines on preparing a research proposal.

Identifying a Population and Selecting a Sample

A *population* is any group in which a researcher is interested. It could be large, such as all undergraduate sociology majors in public universities, or it could be small, such as all students in a college who declared sociology to be their major within the previous academic year.

A *sample* is a subgroup of the population. It is more efficient to study a sample than to study an entire population. Of course, the adequacy of any inferences about a population depends on the adequacy of the method used to select the sample from the population as well as the adequacy of the sample size.

When formulating a research purpose or hypothesis for a term project, it is crucial to consider the accessibility of a suitable population and sample. For instance, if the research purpose is to determine the degree of self-reported depression among high school students and the only way to obtain a sufficient number of high school students is by seeking permission to survey within a high school, a college student planning the survey may find that obtaining permission from the administrators of the high school is a lengthy process that exceeds the student's timeline. Even if time permits, permission may not be granted in the end because of the sensitive nature of the topic. Thus, to complete the term project on time, a purpose or hypothesis for which there is a readily accessible population should be formulated.

Issues in identifying a population and selecting a sample suitable for a term project are described in Chapter 6.

Identifying or Constructing an Instrument

In the social and behavioral sciences, measurement tools such as tests and attitude scales are referred to as *instruments*. For a term project, it is often desirable for students to use instruments that have been professionally developed and refined by others. However, for some research purposes and hypotheses, specialized instruments may be needed, which may require that students build them. In addition, questions soliciting demographic information (i.e., background information such as age and gender) should be included as the main instruments are administered (or administered at the same time).

Techniques for identifying existing instruments are covered in Chapter 7, while basic techniques for constructing new instruments are illustrated in Chapter 8. Devising questions to solicit relevant demographic information is the topic of Chapter 9.

Administering the Instrument

How an instrument is administered can affect the outcome of a survey. For instance, face-to-face administration may yield results on sensitive topics different from an administration that allows participants to respond anonymously. Also, the method of administration (e.g., mailing a questionnaire versus posting it on the Internet) can affect the response rate.

Issues in administering instruments are described in Chapter 10.

Analyzing Data Using Descriptive Statistics

For a basic term-project survey conducted by students with little or no background in statistics, an instructor may require only the use of descriptive statistics (such as averages and percentages) for the data analysis.

The selection of descriptive statistics and the computation of some basic ones are described in Chapters 11, 12, and 13.

Analyzing Data Using Inferential Statistics

Students who have taken one or more courses in statistics may be required to apply inferential statistics in addition to descriptive ones. Inferential statistics apply probability theory to assist in interpreting the data obtained from a sample when making inferences to a population. For instance, margins of error for averages and percentages (e.g., 55% +/– 3% approve of some course of action) are often reported in the results sections of research reports on surveys. The computation of margins of errors for percentages, means, and medians is illustrated in Chapters 11 and 12.

While it is beyond the scope of this book to show the computation of significance tests, Appendix C provides an overview of their purpose.

Preparing a Written Research Report on a Survey

Research reports in the social and behavioral sciences have a standard organization and are written in an academic style. These characteristics are discussed and illustrated in Chapter 14.

Standards for a Term-Project Survey

Standards for a survey conducted as a term project can vary from course to course, depending on course objectives and students' levels of expertise. The following are some basic standards your instructor might consider in evaluating the report of your survey research. He or she may give you feedback on how much emphasis will be placed on each one and may include additional standards for you to consider as you plan and conduct your survey.

1. Appropriateness of the problem area.
2. Suitability of the research purpose and/or hypothesis.
3. Adequacy of the research proposal.
4. Relevance of the literature review.
5. Identification of an appropriate population.
6. Adequate sampling from the population (method of sampling and sample size).
7. Identification or construction of appropriate instruments.
8. Appropriateness of the descriptive statistics in light of the research purpose and/or hypothesis.
9. Appropriate use of inferential statistics (margins of error and significance tests, if required).
10. Adequacy of the written research report in terms of
    A. Organization.
    B. Coherence.
    C. Style, including mechanics such as grammar and spelling.
    D. Proper format for the reference list.

Creating a Timeline for a Term-Project Survey

Because of the limited time frame in which term-project surveys are conducted, a timeline should be drawn up as early as possible, keeping in mind that it can be adjusted as needed along the way. A timeline for basic activities for a semester is illustrated in Example

1.4. Note that more than one activity will be pursued during some weeks. For instance, during Week 5, the literature search and preparing the written review may be ongoing while you are also beginning to write the research proposal.

Example 1.4

A Timeline of Basic Activities for a 16-Week Semester

Week	Identify a topic for a survey	Formulate purpose/ hypothesis	Literature search/write review	Prepare research proposal	Identify/ develop instruments[4]	Admin- ister instru- ments	Analyze data	Write research report/ review and revise
1	XXX							
2	XXX	XXX	XXX					
3		XXX	XXX					
4			XXX					
5			XXX	XXX				
6				XXX	XXX			
7				XXX	XXX			
8					XXX			
9						XXX		
10						XXX		
11						XXX		
12							XXX	
13							XXX	
14							XXX	
15								XXX
16								XXX

When following a timeline, it is a good idea to try to keep ahead of it, which will allow more time for later activities that may be more time-consuming than expected.

Exercise for Chapter 1

1. Reconsider Examples 1.1 and 1.2. In light of the content of the course you are taking, write two original examples in the spaces below. By answering this question, you will *not* be committing to conduct a survey on either research purpose. (A commitment will be made after you complete Chapter 4.) Instead, your answers are for the purposes of class discussion and feedback only. Examine your textbook and course syllabus for ideas.

---

[4] The term "instruments" refers to all measurement tools, such as tests or attitude scales.

Example A

Course title: _____

Broad problem area: _____

Narrower problem area: _____

Research purpose for a survey: _____

_____

Example B

Course title: _____

Broad problem area: _____

Narrower problem area: _____

Research purpose for a survey: _____

_____

2. Write a research hypothesis for each of the two examples in Question 1. (Note that you will learn more about formulating hypotheses in Chapter 3.) Your answers to this question are for discussion purposes only and may help you and other students begin thinking about possible hypotheses that might be explored with a survey.

Research hypothesis related to Example A in Question 1:

_____

_____

Research hypothesis related to Example B in Question 1:

_____

_____

3. Will you be following the timeline in Example 1.4? If your semester or quarter has more or fewer weeks than the 16 in the example, prepare a revised timeline on a separate piece of paper.

Chapter 2

Identifying a Topic for a Survey

As indicated in Chapter 1, the first step in conducting a survey is to identify several broad problem areas and get feedback from other students and the instructor on their suitability. After selecting an area, it should be narrowed so that it is manageable as the basis for a term-project survey. The narrow problem area can be thought of as the "topic" for the survey.

This chapter is designed to help students identify topic ideas for term-project surveys. Many of the examples in this chapter refer to college students as participants because they are often the most accessible participants for individuals conducting a survey as a term project.

Topics Related to Scientific Theories

As indicated in Chapter 1, the term *scientific theory* is used in this book to refer to any theory that has two characteristics: (a) it has been described in academic publications such as journals, and (b) it has at least some empirical support as indicated by published research attesting to its validity.

Example 2.1 briefly describes one aspect of attachment theory and a possible topic for a survey based on the theory.

Example 2.1

A topic for a survey based on attachment theory:

Brief, partial description of the theory:

Attachment theory portrays individuals "...as motivated to maintain real or imagined proximity to safety- and security-providing attachment figures (i.e., caregivers), especially in periods of stress and distress." Having secure attachments "allows individuals to function autonomously and pursue other important goals, such as exploration, affiliation, and sexual mating, that foster growth, adaptation...."[1]

Possible survey topic based on the theory:

A survey to examine whether college students who have recently experienced stressful events report initiating more contacts with their parents than students who have not recently experienced stressful events.

---

[1] Hart, J., Shaver, P. R., & Goldenberg, J. L. (2005). Attachment, self-esteem, worldviews, and terror management: Evidence for a tripartite security system. *Journal of Personality and Social Psychology, 88,* 999–1013.

Example 2.2 briefly describes one aspect of dominance theory and a possible topic for a survey based on the theory.

Example 2.2

A topic for a survey based on dominance theory:

Brief, partial description of the theory:

"The dominance theory of gender-linked language differences suggest that men's domination of conversations via interruption and topic introduction is reflective of the power they hold in larger society. From this perspective, men use questions, interruptions, and other means of communication as a way to dominate conversation and to keep women in a subordinate position."[2]

Possible survey topic based on the theory:

A survey of college women to determine their perspectives on their conversations with men and women, specifically, to compare how each woman perceives selected aspects of conversations with her best male friend and her best female friend.

Example 2.3 briefly describes one aspect of self-discrepancy theory and a possible topic for a survey based on the theory.

Example 2.3

A topic for a survey based on self-discrepancy theory:

Brief, partial description of the theory:

Self-discrepancy theory "proposes that within an individual's self-concept are causal factors for anxiety, depression, body dissatisfaction, and eating-disordered behavior."[3] Among other things, the theory addresses possible discrepancies between the actual self-concept and the ideal self-concept that individuals possess.

Possible survey topic based on the theory:

A survey to examine whether college students who have large discrepancies between their actual self-concept and ideal self-concept report more anxiety in social situations.

Most college textbooks in content areas discuss major theories. In addition, less well-known theories that might be used as a basis for a term project can be identified through a literature search, which is illustrated in Chapter 4.

Box 2A shows a sample of theories in the social and behavioral sciences. Examining studies that explore these theories (identified through a literature search using the names of

---

[2] Werner-Wilson, R. J., Murphy, M. J., & Fitzharris, L. (2004). Does therapist experience influence interruptions of women clients? *Journal of Feminist Family Therapy, 16,* 39–49.

[3] Halliwell, E., & Dittmar, H. (2006). Associations between appearance-related self-discrepancies and young women's and men's affect, body satisfaction, and emotional eating: A comparison of fixed-item and participant-generated self-discrepancies. *Personality and Social Psychology Bulletin, 32,* 447–458.

each theory as a search term) can provide useful ideas for topics for surveys. One recent reference for each is given in footnotes at the bottom of this page.

Box 2A   *A sample of theories in the social and behavior sciences.*

1. Social Learning Theory[4]

2. Theory of Planned Behavior[5]

3. Reversal Theory[6]

4. Cognitive Information Processing Theory[7]

5. Control Theory[8]

6. Threshold Theory[9]

7. Shame Resilience Theory[10]

8. Theory of Reciprocity[11]

9. Social Cognitive Career Theory[12]

10. Theory of Motivated Information Management[13]

11. Status Characteristics Theory[14]

12. Social Schema Theory[15]

---

[4] Read, J. P., & O'Connor, R. M. (2006). High- and low-dose expectancies as mediators of personality dimensions and alcohol involvement. *Journal of Studies on Alcohol, 67,* 204–214.

[5] Chatzisarantis, N. L. D., Hagger, M. S., Smith, B., & Sage, L. D. (2006). The influences of intrinsic motivation on execution of social behaviour within the theory of planned behaviour. *European Journal of Social Psychology, 36,* 229–237.

[6] Shepherd, D. J., Lee, B., & Kerr, J. H. (2006). Reversal theory: A suggested way forward for an improved understanding of interpersonal relationships in sport. *Psychology of Sport and Exercise, 7,* 143–157.

[7] Osborn, D. S., & Reardon, R. C. (2006). Using the self-directed search: Career explorer with high-risk middle school students. *Career Development Quarterly, 54,* 269–273.

[8] Costello, B. J., Anderson, B. J., & Stein, M. D. (2006). Heavy episodic drinking among adolescents: a test of hypotheses derived from control theory. *Journal of Alcohol and Drug Education, 50,* 35–55.

[9] Preckel, F., Holling, H., & Wiese, M. (2006). Relationship of intelligence and creativity in gifted and non-gifted students: An investigation of threshold theory. *Personality and Individual Differences, 40,* 159–170.

[10] Brown, B. (2006). Shame resilience theory: A grounded theory study on women and shame. *Families in Society, 87,* 43–52.

[11] Falk, A., & Fischbacher, U. (2006). A theory of reciprocity. *Games and Economic Behavior, 54,* 293–315.

[12] Betz, N. E., & Hackett, G. (2006). Career self-efficacy theory: Back to the future. *Journal of Career Assessment, 14,* 3–11.

[13] Afifi, W. A., & Weiner, J. L. (2006). Seeking information about sexual health: Applying the theory of motivated information management. *Human Communication Research, 32,* 35–57.

[14] Gaughan, M. (2006). The gender structure of adolescent peer influence on drinking. *Journal of Health and Social Behavior, 47,* 47–61.

[15] Nesdale, D., & Pickering, K. (2006). Teachers' reactions to children's aggression. *Social Development, 15,* 109–127.

Topics Related to Programs and Services

It is common to conduct surveys to determine individuals' reactions to services and programs. A "service" is an activity that is narrow in scope such as a translation service for foreign exchange students, while a "program" is broader, consisting of coordinated services (such as an academic assistance program for foreign exchange students, which might consist of a variety of services such as personal and academic counseling, English instruction, academic tutoring, and so on). Obviously, a survey on a service will tend to be narrower in focus than a survey on a formal program with many components.

Surveys Relating to Existing Services and Programs

Many potential topics can be generated by considering the delivery of services by existing programs. For instance, most colleges have job-placement programs. A survey might be conducted to evaluate the satisfaction of students currently using such a program (e.g., current students' satisfaction with the number of career counselors available to assist students, hours of operation, ease of making appointments with program personnel, and so on). A survey might also be conducted to evaluate such a program from the point of view of students who have already used the program (e.g., graduated students' satisfaction with the usefulness of the program in helping them find employment).[16] Box 2B shows a sample of services and programs that might be explored with a survey.

When considering existing services and programs as areas for topics for a survey, it is important to consider accessibility to the program providers and recipients. For instance, an employed teacher taking a master's level graduate course might be able to survey students in a program in a public school, while other types of students might find such access difficult to obtain.

Box 2B   *A sample of services and programs that might be explored in a survey.*

---

1. Social support services for freshmen residing on a college campus.

2. After-school tutoring in math in a public school setting.

3. Educational programs offered by a hospital for individuals with diabetes.

4. Services offered by a probation department for first-time offenders.

5. Community-outreach programs sponsored by a police department.

6. College library reference room services for college freshmen.

---

[16] In the field of program evaluation, evaluation of the delivery of services is called a *formative evaluation*, while evaluation of outcomes attributable to the services is called a *summative evaluation*.

Surveys Relating to Potential Services and Programs

Surveys are sometimes conducted for the practical purpose of determining the need for new services and programs. For instance, a survey might be conducted to determine the needs of individuals with physical handicaps for additional access to college facilities. Surveys conducted for this type of purpose are often called "needs assessments."

Topics Related to Product Satisfaction

Surveys are useful for obtaining users' reactions to and opinions on products. For instance, a survey might be conducted on college students' opinions on competing products such as educational software programs, with an emphasis on identifying the distinguishing characteristics of the programs that make them appealing.

Topics Related to Knowledge

Using tests, a term-project survey can be used to assess individuals' knowledge. Two possibilities are described below.

Surveys Relating to Knowledge of Practical Information

"Practical information" is defined here as information that might directly impact the decisions and behaviors of individuals in their everyday lives. Individuals with correct information should be better able to make sound decisions and engage in appropriate behaviors, while those with little information or misinformation might be less well equipped to do so.

An example of a survey of practical knowledge would be a survey of college students' knowledge of the legal consequences of driving under the influence of alcohol (e.g., fines, possible jail time, and legal fees). If a survey revealed a deficit in such information among a group of college students, a practical implication would be for college personnel to improve education on this topic.

Surveys Relating to Knowledge of Professional Standards

Each profession has standards for the conduct of members of the profession. Such standards are often published by professional associations as well as by legislators and boards that issue licenses. Knowledge of such standards can be the basis for a term-project survey. For instance, a survey could be conducted on graduate students' knowledge of the ethical principles described in the *Professional Conduct Manual* of the National Association of School Psychologists.

Topics Related to Behaviors

Asking respondents about their behaviors using a survey can yield valuable information.

Surveys Relating to Current Behaviors

Survey topics often focus on problem behaviors and/or behaviors that have the potential for harm. For instance, surveys can be conducted on problem drinking, problem gambling, and illicit drug use. While a survey can be conducted to estimate only the incidence of such behaviors in a particular population, surveys can be informative when the incidence in two or more contrasting groups is examined. For instance, a survey designed to compare the incidence of binge drinking by students who belong to fraternities with students who do not belong to fraternities may help in understanding the context in which the behaviors occur.

A term-project survey can also be used to study behaviors that are beneficial. For instance, high-achieving students might be surveyed to explore their work habits related to academic activities such as preparing for classroom tests.

Surveys Relating to Self-Reported Reasons for Behavior

In addition to examining the incidence of behaviors among members of selected groups, a term-project survey can be used to examine the reasons participants give for engaging in certain behaviors. For instance, a survey might be conducted in which respondents are asked for their reasons for selecting sociology as a major or for their reasons for avoiding certain types of coursework.

Topics Related to Attitudes and Opinions

While the terms *attitudes* and *opinions* are sometimes used interchangeably, in this book, a distinction is made. Specifically, an *attitude* is defined as a relatively stable general predisposition toward some entity (e.g., attitude toward the Republican party), while an *opinion* generally is more focused and potentially more transient (e.g., opinion on a particular Republican candidate for president).

Surveys Relating to Political Opinions and Attitudes

Professional polling agencies are often commissioned to conduct surveys on political issues and candidates. The results can help politicians mold potential political actions so that they are maximally acceptable to the public. For term-project surveys, students might conduct surveys on current political topics on campuses (e.g., surveys relating to college elections and to the operation of elected boards on college campuses), with attention to how various subgroups (e.g., freshmen) differ in their opinions and attitudes from other subgroups (e.g., seniors).

Surveys Relating to Nonpolitical Opinions and Attitudes

In addition to political attitudes, surveys often examine nonpolitical attitudes that may have practical implications for policy makers, educators, and other professionals. Examples of topics for attitude surveys are attitudes toward the mainstream television news media, attitudes toward gender equality, and attitudes toward organized religion. As with surveys on political opinions and attitudes, examining how various subgroups differ can provide interesting contrasts.

Topics Suggested in the Literature

Chapter 4 deals with locating published literature. This should be done as soon as possible because examining previous studies can often provide guidance for surveys that may be conducted as a term project.

Surveys Based on Suggestions for Future Research

Researchers who publish research in academic journals often make suggestions for extending their work in future research. Example 2.4 shows a suggestion that appeared at the end of a report on a survey regarding how interns and training directors perceive the quality of multicultural training at their internship sites.

Example 2.4

A topic for a survey suggested at the end of a published survey on multicultural training:

"Finally, because the items…used in this study were related to multiculturalism regarding racial and ethnic issues only, other aspects of culture, including sexuality, religion, disability status, age, and gender issues, were not examined. Future studies examining these other components of culture are in order."[17]

Example 2.5 shows a suggestion that appeared at the end of a report on a survey regarding how teachers work with struggling writers.

Example 2.5

A topic for a survey suggested at the end of a published survey on adaptations teachers make when working with struggling writers:

"In future investigations it may be more productive to key teacher adaptations to individual students, rather than struggling writers as a group, as was done in the present study. It may also be important to distinguish between routine adaptations (i.e.,

---

[17] Magyar-Moe, J. L., Pedrotti, J. T., Edwards, L. M., Ford, A. I., Petersen, S. E., Rasmussen, H. N., & Ryder, J. A. (2005). Perceptions of multicultural training in predoctoral internship programs: A survey of interns and training directors. *Professional Psychology: Research and Practice, 36*, 446–450.

planned modifications in established classroom routines) and specialized adaptations (i.e., unanticipated modifications introduced when students respond poorly)...."[18]

Surveys Based on Suggestions for Improving Current Research

With hindsight, researchers often indicate how the research they are reporting could have been improved. For a term-project survey, a student might replicate the published study while improving on the methodology as suggested by the author of a previous survey. Example 2.6 shows a suggestion for an improvement in a replication. It appeared in a published survey on the role of psychology in hospitals.

Example 2.6

A suggestion for a modification in a replication made in a published survey:

"It is therefore recommended that although a future survey might wish to use the same methodology as...the current study, items should be added to the survey to reflect more contemporary hospital practice and terminology."[19]

Ethical Issues in Topic Selection

Researchers are obliged to treat the participants in their research ethically and protect them from harm.

Protection from Harm

While the typical procedures in conducting surveys (e.g., mailing a questionnaire) seldom pose physical hazards to participants, the topics of some surveys can pose two types of psychological hazards.

First, questions on sensitive topics (e.g., child sexual abuse) may cause psychological respondents to experience distress, even extreme distress. Thus, students planning a survey as a term project usually should avoid sensitive topics, leaving this work to professional researchers who are knowledgeable in how to deal with the ethical issues they pose.

Second, psychological harm can result from careless handling of data, which might result in the confidentiality of the individuals' responses being compromised. If the responses are collected anonymously (e.g., with no identifying information on questionnaires), confidentiality becomes less of an issue.

---

[18] Graham, S., Harris, K. R., Fink-Chorzempa, B., & MacArthur, C. (2003). Primary grade teachers' instructional adaptations for struggling writers: A national survey. *Journal of Educational Psychology, 95,* 279–292.

[19] Humbke, K. L., Brown, D. L., Welder, A. N., Fillion, D. T., Dobson, K. S., & Arnett, J. L. (2004). A survey of hospital psychology in Canada. *Canadian Psychology, 45,* 31–41.

Informed Consent

By informing potential participants of the purpose of a survey and making sure they understand they are free to refuse to participate without penalties, a researcher can avoid many ethical issues. Informed consent should usually be obtained in writing. Colleges have policies on how to obtain such consent and have committees that review proposed consent procedures, as well as assess whether research procedures might harm participants. When selecting a topic, consider whether potential participants will likely consent to take part in a survey on the topic, as well as whether the committee will be likely to give approval for the research.

Exercise for Chapter 2

1. Brainstorm possible topics for term-project surveys in as many of the following areas as possible and share your ideas with other students who may get ideas for topics for their own term projects. Attempt to identify topics that would be manageable to use as the basis for surveys as term projects by students with limited resources.

   A. Topics related to scientific theories.

   B. Topics related to programs and services.

   C. Topics related to product satisfaction.

   D. Topics related to knowledge.

   E. Topics related to behaviors.

   F. Topics related to attitudes and opinions.

2. Are you aware of any published studies that contain suggestions for future research and/or for improving current research? If yes, describe them here.

3. Are you aware of any guidelines your college has regarding ethical issues in conducting research? If yes, briefly describe them here.

Chapter 3

Formulating Research Purposes

As indicated in Chapter 1, the first step in conducting a survey is to identify several broad problem areas and get feedback from other students and the instructor on their suitability. Then, the broad problem area should be narrowed to a specific topic (see Chapter 2) so that it is manageable as the basis for a term-project survey. Next, a specific research purpose should be formulated.

After working through this chapter, you should have several possible research purposes. A final selection and revision of the purposes should not be made until the literature on the topic has been examined. Locating and synthesizing literature on a topic is covered in the next two chapters. These activities may yield information that could lead to revision of the tentative purposes or even the rejection of the tentative purposes in favor of others that might be more fruitful for a term project.

Essential Characteristics of a Specific Research Purpose

To qualify as a specific research purpose, the purpose should (a) refer to at least one population[1] and (b) name at least one variable. A variable is a trait or characteristic of the population. In Example 3.1, the population consists of "adolescents," and the variable is "attitudes toward smoking tobacco."

Example 3.1

A research purpose with one population and one variable:

The purpose is to determine adolescents' attitudes toward smoking tobacco.

In Example 3.2, the population consists of "college students," and the variable is "knowledge of the consequences of binge drinking."

Example 3.2

A research purpose with one population and one variable:

The purpose is to determine college students' knowledge of the consequences of binge drinking.

Research Purposes with More Than One Population

In Example 3.3, there is one variable (knowledge of the consequences of binge drinking). However, there are two populations: (a) freshmen undergraduates and (b) senior under-

---

[1] Although a research purpose refers to a population, a sample from the population may be used when conducting the survey.

graduates. Note that when there is more than one population, the purpose is usually to compare the populations. To keep a term project manageable, the number of populations should be limited.

Example 3.3

A research purpose with two populations and one variable:

The purpose is to compare freshmen and senior undergraduates' knowledge of the consequences of binge drinking.

Research Purposes with More Than One Variable

In Example 3.4, there is one population (college students). However, there are two variables: (a) "knowledge of HIV transmission" and (b) "attitudes toward individuals with HIV." To keep a term project manageable, the number of variables should be limited.

Example 3.4

A research purpose with one population and two variables (no relationship specified):

The purpose is to determine college students' knowledge of HIV transmission and their attitudes toward individuals with HIV.

When there are two variables, researchers are often interested in the relationship between the two. If this is the case, the purpose should indicate that a relationship will be examined. Example 3.5 shows how this might be done.

Example 3.5

A research purpose with one population and two variables (relationship specified):

The purpose is to estimate the degree of relationship between college students' knowledge of HIV transmission and their attitudes toward individuals with HIV.

A Wide Variety of Populations and Variables in Research Purposes

There is an almost infinite number of populations and variables (as well as combinations) that might be used in a research purpose. Box 3A shows some that have been examined in recently published surveys in a variety of fields.[2] Note that for each example in the box, the number of populations and variables are indicated in parentheses. Studying these may help in learning how to state research purposes involving one or more populations and one or more variables.

The data resulting from a survey involving only one population and one variable will typically be easier to analyze statistically than data from a survey using multiple populations and variables. However, the latter may provide more interesting results. Instructors may pro-

---

[2] The purposes in Box 3A have been simplified from the originals for instructional purposes.

vide guidance on the suitability of using multiple populations and variables in a term project for the class in which this book is being used.

Box 3A   *A sample of research purposes explored in recently published surveys.*

---

1. To determine which treatments for autism are used by parents of children with autism.[3] (*One population; one variable*)

2. To examine the relationship between the importance undergraduates attribute to attendance and the rates at which they subsequently attend class.[4] (*One population; one variable*)

3. To estimate teachers' knowledge about epilepsy and their attitudes toward students with epilepsy.[5] (*One population; two variables*)

4. To survey critical care nurses to obtain suggestions for improving end-of-life care and to determine their perceptions of the barriers to providing good deaths.[6] (*One population; two variables*)

5. To examine adults' willingness to drop off e-waste at recycling centers in relation to their gender and environmental beliefs.[7] (*One population; three variables*)

6. To assess adults' (a) exposure to a statewide advertising campaign for increasing awareness of problem gambling, (b) views on problem gambling campaigns in general, and (c) knowledge of problem gambling.[8] (*One population; three variables*)

7. To determine the frequency of use of alternative medical therapies by Chinese and Vietnamese Americans.[9] (*Two populations; one variable*)

(Continued on next page)

---

[3] Green, V. A., Pituch, K. A., Itchon, J., Choi, A., O'Reilly, M., & Sigafoos, J. (2006). Internet survey of treatments used by parents of children with autism. *Research in Developmental Disabilities, 27*, 70–84.

[4] Gump, S. E. (2006). Guess who's (not) coming to class: Student attitudes as indicators of attendance. *Educational Studies, 32*, 39–46.

[5] Bishop, M., & Boag, E. M. (2006). Teachers' knowledge about epilepsy and attitudes toward students with epilepsy: Results of a national survey. *Epilepsy & Behavior, 8*, 397–405.

[6] Beckstrand, R. L., Callister, L. C., & Kirchhoff, K. T. (2006). Providing a "good death": Critical care nurses' suggestions for improving end-of-life care. *American Journal of Critical Care, 15*, 38–46.

[7] Saphores, J.-D. M., Nixon, H., Ogunseitan, O. A., & Shapiro, A. A. (2006). Household willingness to recycle electronic waste: An application to California. *Environment and Behavior, 38*, 183–208.

[8] Najavits, L. M., Grymala, L. D., & George, B. (2003). Can advertising increase awareness of problem gambling? A statewide survey of impact. *Psychology of Addictive Behaviors, 17*, 324–327.

[9] Ahn, A. C., Ngo-Metzger, Q., Legedza, A. T. R., Massagli, M. P., Clarridge, B. R., & Phillips, R. S. (2006). Complementary and alternative medical therapy use among Chinese and Vietnamese Americans: Prevalence, associated factors, and effects of patient–clinician communication. *American Journal of Public Health, 96*, 647–653.

Box 3A *Continued.*

8. To measure the impact of the September 11th attacks on adolescent students and their teachers.[10] (*Two populations*; *one variable*)

9. To survey school counselors in New York and school counselors in Colorado to estimate (a) their comfort with technology and (b) their use of technology in counseling.[11] (*Two populations*; *two variables*)

Research Purposes Stated As Questions

A research purpose can be stated in the form of a research question. For instance, consider Example 3.6, which shows the research purpose in Example 3.1 rewritten as a question.

Example 3.6
A research purpose and corresponding research question:

The research purpose in Example 3.1:

The purpose is to determine adolescents' attitudes toward smoking tobacco.

The research purpose in Example 3.1 stated as a question:

What are adolescents' attitudes toward smoking tobacco?

Example 3.7 shows the research purpose in Example 3.5 rewritten as a question.

Example 3.7
A research purpose and corresponding research question:

The research purpose in Example 3.5:

The purpose is to estimate the degree of relationship between college students' knowledge of HIV transmission and their attitudes toward individuals with HIV.

The research purpose in Example 3.5 restated as a question:

What is the degree of relationship between college students' knowledge of HIV transmission and their attitudes toward individuals with HIV?

Using Care in Stating a Yes–No Research Question

Generally, research questions should *not* be in a form that implies the answer to the question will be either "yes" or "no." This is because the results of surveys are almost always more complex than a simple yes–no answer. For instance, consider Example 3.8. The yes–no

---

[10] Noppe, I. C., Noppe, L. D., & Bartell, D. (2006). Terrorism and resilience: Adolescents' and teachers' responses to September 11, 2001. *Death Studies*, *30*, 41–60.

[11] Carlson, L. A., Portman, T. A. A., & Bartlett, J. R. (2006). Professional school counselors' approaches to technology. *Professional School Counseling*, *9*, 252–256.

version implies that the answer that will be found in the research will be a simple "yes" or "no," while in all likelihood the answer will be *some degree* of difference (e.g., 40% of one group opposes the death penalty while 45% of the other group does). The improved version in Example 3.8 accommodates this type of intermediate (not black-and-white) result.

Example 3.8
A yes–no research question and its improved version:

A yes–no research question:

Are there differences in opinions on the death penalty between college students who hold strong religious values and students who do not hold such values?

An improved version of the question:

To what extent do students who hold strong religious values differ in their opinions on the death penalty from students who do not hold such values?

Choosing Between the Statement Form and Question Form

A basic research purpose is stated in the form of a declarative statement. As indicated above, it can also be stated in the form of a question. Whether to use a declarative statement or a question is a matter of personal preference. Neither form is inherently superior to the other.

Research Purposes Stated As Hypotheses

A hypothesis is a statement that predicts the outcome of the study. Students who have some basis for predicting the outcome of the survey they are planning may state their research purpose in the form of a hypothesis.

Directional Hypotheses

A *directional hypothesis* indicates the type of difference or relationship that is predicted. Example 3.9 predicts the type of difference expected.

Example 3.9
A directional hypothesis that predicts the type of difference expected:

It is hypothesized that first- and second-generation American college students have more liberal attitudes regarding immigration policies than third- and older-generation students.

Example 3.10 illustrates a directional hypothesis that indicates the type of relationship the researcher expects to find.

Example 3.10
A directional hypothesis that predicts the direction of a relationship:

It is hypothesized that there is a direct relationship between public school teachers' attitudes toward statewide achievement testing and the abilities of their students, with teachers who have higher-achieving students also having more positive attitudes.

Nondirectional Hypotheses

A nondirectional hypothesis indicates that there is a difference or relationship, but it does not indicate the type of difference expected (i.e., does not indicate the direction of the difference or relationship). Example 3.11 illustrates a nondirectional hypothesis.

Example 3.11
A nondirectional hypothesis:

It is hypothesized that students who live on campus report a different level of satisfaction with their social lives than students who live off campus.

Note that nondirectional hypotheses are less common than directional ones. This is because researchers who anticipate a difference or relationship usually have some sense of its direction.

Exercise for Chapter 3

Directions: Share your answers to this exercise with other students who may still be trying to identify a topic for their term projects.

1. Write an original research purpose that names more than one population but only one variable. It should be "original" in the sense that it is not one that you have seen in print before; it does *not* need to exhibit "creative originality." State the purpose as a statement—not in the form of a question.

2. Write an original research purpose that names only one population but has two or more variables. State the purpose as a statement—not in the form of a question.

3. Rewrite your answer to either Question 1 or 2 as a question. Which of the two versions do you prefer? Why?

4. Is your research question in response to Question 3 in the form of a yes–no question? If it is, is this desirable? Explain.

5. Write an original directional research hypothesis.

6. Write an original nondirectional research hypothesis.

7. Do you plan to pursue any of the purposes stated in Questions 1 through 6 as the basis for your term project?

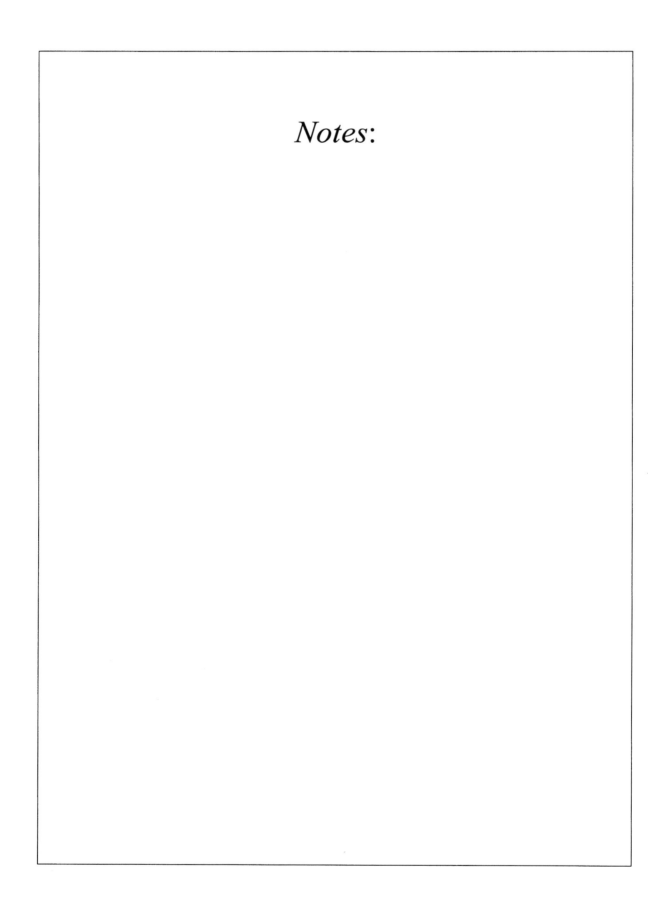

Notes:

Chapter 4

Locating Related Literature

Examining published research on a potential research topic can help in identifying and refining a research purpose for a term-project survey.

Note that research reports in journals are almost always the *primary source* (i.e., original source) of research findings. Reports of research in books and nonacademic periodicals such as weekly newsmagazines are almost always secondary sources, which are typically brief and may be oversimplified. As a consequence, the primary sources in journals should be emphasized by students conducting term-project surveys.

Basics for Searching Electronic Literature Databases

Searching for literature published in journals is facilitated by electronic databases that allow users to search a wide variety of journals for research related to their topics.

Using a Thesaurus

Major databases maintain a thesaurus of descriptors (i.e., terms used for classifying the materials in the database). By using the descriptors identified in a thesaurus, a user can conduct a more efficient search of the literature.

The example below illustrates how users can start with a very broad term and then identify narrow descriptors that focus on particular aspects of the broad term.

Consider the *ERIC* Database, sponsored by the U.S. Department of Education. At the time of this writing, it is located at www.eric.ed.gov and can be accessed by any Internet user free of charge. On the home page, there is a tab at the top for the "Thesaurus." Clicking on it produces the screen shown in Figure 4.1 on the next page. As you can see, it allows users to browse the Thesaurus alphabetically or by category (broad topic). Clicking on a category produces additional categories, each of which can be used as a descriptor in an *ERIC* search. Note that the Thesaurus does not lead directly to references to journal articles. Instead, it provides assistance in identifying descriptors that might be productive in searching the database.

In addition to browsing by clicking on the categories in Figure 4.1, a search term can be entered to the right of "Search for." Suppose a student is interested in the broad topic of multicultural issues. Typing in the word "multicultural" in the search box (as indicated by the arrow) and then clicking on the "Search" tab just below the space where "multicultural" was typed, brings up five more narrow descriptors shown in Figure 4.2: Multicultural Education, Multicultural Literature (2004), Multicultural Textbooks, Multicultural Training, and Multiculturalism.

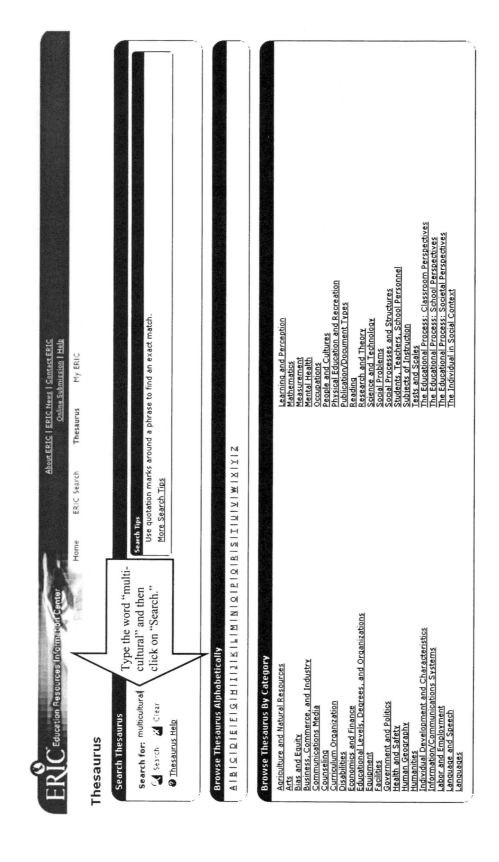

Figure 4.1. ERIC Database screen after the Thesaurus tab has been clicked.

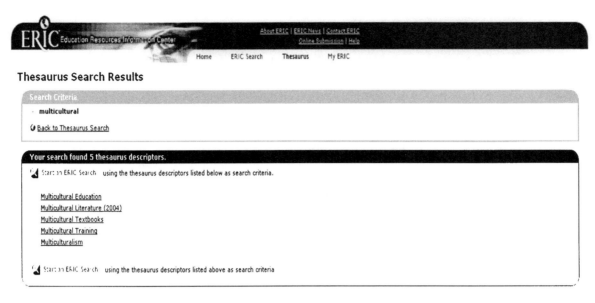

Figure 4.2. ERIC Database screen as a result of a search for the term "multicultural."

Clicking on "Multicultural Education" (the first descriptor in the list in Figure 4.2) produces the descriptors related to multicultural education shown in Figure 4.3. Each of these related descriptors represents a more narrow aspect of multicultural education. Using these descriptors in a search of the *ERIC* database allows a user to conduct a focused and, hence, a more efficient search.

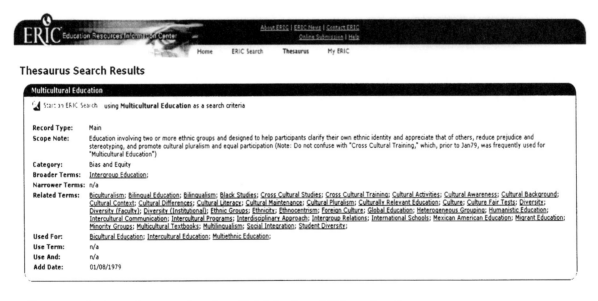

Figure 4.3. Descriptors related to "Multicultural Education."

Quick Search versus Advanced or Fielded Search

After consulting a thesaurus to identify appropriate descriptors, go back to the home page of the database to begin a search for literature.

On the home page of major electronic databases, there is often a "quick search" box. A descriptor can be entered in this box to conduct a search that identifies all literature related to the descriptor. However, a more focused search can be conducted by first clicking on the link for an "Advanced Search" (also sometimes called a "Fielded Search"). In the advanced search mode, a user may be able to specify the types of publications (e.g., journals only), the relevant dates of publications, and to use Boolean operators, which are described below.

Figure 4.4 shows the fielded search screen for the *PsycINFO* database, maintained by the American Psychological Association (www.apa.org).[1] Notice that the default is to search only journals (indicated by the check mark to the left of the word "Journals"). Also notice that the default is for literature published in the last three years, which can be changed by typing in the desired years.

Using Boolean Operators

Boolean operators can be used to search using various combinations of descriptors. In the *PsycINFO* database, the Boolean operators are "and," "or," and "not."

In the fielded search screen for *PsycINFO* in Figure 4.4, the operator "and" is the default (see the arrow). The operator "and" indicates that the user wants to identify only articles that contain both descriptors. For instance, in Figure 4.4, the descriptors "race" and "college" have been entered under "Look for." At the time of this writing, this search identified 679 articles, each of which contains the descriptors race *and* college.[2]

By clicking on the down arrowhead to the right of the word "and," the Boolean operator can be changed to "or," which will identify all articles that contain *either* the word "race" or "college." At the time of this writing, this search produced 33,605 articles. Clearly, this would not be a productive search strategy for a student seeking literature on these two variables because such a large number of articles have been identified.

---

[1] Large academic libraries usually subscribe to this database and make it available to students free of charge.
[2] If only "race" is searched for, 3,539 journal articles are identified. Using "race" AND "college" greatly reduces the number of articles identified.

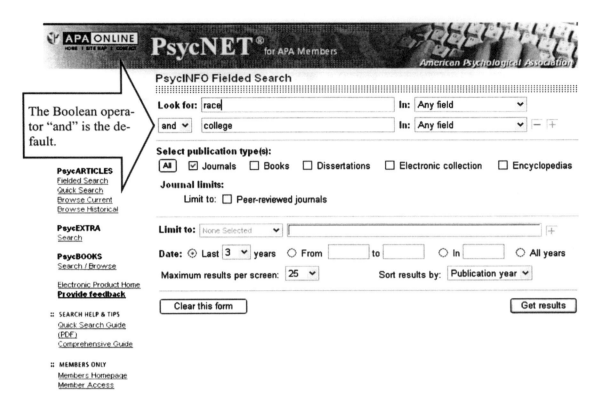

Figure 4.4. PsycINFO "fielded search" screen with the descriptors "race" and "college" entered.

The third Boolean operator on the drop-down menu where "and" appears in Figure 4.4 is "not." Using "not" eliminates journal articles that include the second descriptor. For instance, using "race" NOT "children" produces all journal articles including race after *eliminating* all that also include children. This search strategy would be helpful for a user who wants to study racial issues only among adolescents and adults.

Special Techniques for Searching Electronic Literature Databases

Below are some techniques that will help produce a focused search of an electronic database.

Using "Survey" As a Descriptor

Suppose a student is considering conducting a survey on smoking behavior. Searching using only the descriptor "smoking" in the *PsycINFO* database at the time of this writing yields 4,107 journal articles, most of which are not surveys. To limit the search to surveys on smoking, using "smoking" AND "survey" as descriptors yields a more limited 702 journal articles.

While it is not necessary to limit a literature search for a term-project survey to previously published surveys, locating and examining previous surveys is helpful in locating instruments (e.g., questionnaires) that might be used in the term-project survey. Also, using "survey" as a search term is especially helpful to students who are trying to identify previous surveys that might be replicated in a term project. The possibility of replication is discussed in Chapters 1 and 2.

Using "Theory" as a Descriptor

Suppose a student is considering conducting a survey on smoking and wants to conduct a survey based on a scientific theory, as discussed in the previous chapter. Using the word "theory" as one of the search descriptors can help identify previous studies on smoking in which one or more theories are discussed. For instance, at the time of this writing, using "smoking" AND "theory" as descriptors yields 330 journal articles containing both descriptors.

Using Fields to Find the Most Relevant Articles

Notice that in Figure 4.4, the default in the upper-right corner is "Any field." All searches mentioned earlier in this chapter searched for the search descriptors anywhere in any part (i.e., any field) of the articles. If such a search yields too many articles, restricting the search to the "Abstract" field can be helpful. An abstract is a summary of a journal article, which usually appears near the beginning of the article. An article in which a descriptor is used in the abstract is more likely to focus on that descriptor than an article in which the descriptor may be mentioned coincidentally in the body of the article.

Consider a student who has searched for "smoking" and "theory" in any field and has retrieved references to 330 journal articles. If "Any field" in Figure 4.4 is changed to the "abstract" field by clicking on the down-arrowhead to the right of "Any field" and selecting "abstract," the number of articles is reduced to 98. These 98 articles all have the words "smoking" and "theory" in their abstracts.

Even more limited results can be obtained by changing "Any field" to the "title" field. For instance, searching for articles that have both "smoking" and "theory" in their titles yields only 14 articles. Articles that have both these descriptors in their titles are most likely to be relevant in identifying theory-based studies of smoking. Box 4A on the next page shows the titles of some of the 14 articles that were identified in this way.

To summarize, using "Any field" identifies articles that have the descriptors anywhere in the articles. Searching using the "abstract" field or "title" field will produce fewer articles that are likely to be more closely focused on the descriptors than a search in "Any field."

Box 4A *Five of the 14 journal articles identified by searching for "smoking" and "theory" in the title field only.*

1. Smoking among adolescents in China: An analysis based upon the meanings of smoking theory. *American Journal of Health Promotion*

2. Quitting smoking: Applying an extended version of the theory of planned behavior to predict intention and behavior. *Journal of Applied Biobehavioral Research*

3. Using an extended theory of planned behavior to understand smoking among schoolchildren. *Addiction Research and Theory*

4. Theory-based determinants of youth smoking: A multiple influence approach. *Journal of Applied Social Psychology*

5. Reversal theory states and cigarette availability predict lapses during smoking cessation among adolescents. *Research in Nursing & Health*

Selected Electronic Databases

While the use of only two databases (*ERIC* and *PsycINFO*) have been illustrated in this chapter, note that there are many other electronic databases, some of which are broad in their coverage (see Box 4B for a sample) and some of which are very narrow in their focus (see Box 4C for a sample). A reference librarian can provide information on which ones are most relevant to your research topic as well as which ones can be accessed free of charge through an account with the library.

Box 4B *A sample of major electronic databases that are broad in their coverage within academic disciplines.*

1. *ERIC* in education.

2. *PsycINFO* and *PsycARTICLES* in psychology.

3. *Sociological Abstracts* in sociology.

4. *Social Work Abstracts* in social work.

5. *Criminal Justice Abstracts* in criminal justice.

6. *CINAHL* in nursing and allied health.

7. *ABI/INFORM* in business and management.

8. *SPORT Discus* in sports medicine and physical education.

9. *Academic Search Premier* in a wide variety of disciplines.

Box 4C   *A sample of specialized electronic databases that are narrow in their coverage.*

1. *GenderWatch* across disciplines.

2. *Alt Health Watch* for alternative and complementary medical issues.

3. *Chicano Abstracts* across disciplines.

4. *Women's Studies International* in feminist research.

5. *Health Source: Nursing/Academic Edition* in nursing and related fields.

Exercise for Chapter 4

Directions: After you have conducted a search using an electronic database to search for research reports in journals, answer the following questions.

1. What is the name of the database you used?

2. Does the database have a thesaurus? Did you use it? Was it useful in helping you identify relevant descriptors? Explain.

3. Did you use Boolean operators? If yes, which one(s)? Did using them help you narrow your search? Explain.

4. Did you use the term "survey" as one of the descriptors? If yes, was it helpful in identifying previous surveys on your topic? Explain.

5. Did you use the term "theory" as one of the descriptors? If yes, was it helpful in identifying theory-based research on your topic? Explain.

6. Did you try restricting your search to the abstract and/or title fields? If yes, was this a useful search strategy for you? Explain.

Chapter 5

Writing a Literature Review

An effective literature review synthesizes the literature on a topic. In most short research reports and research proposals, the literature review serves as the introduction. In other words, the literature review introduces the research topic and helps readers understand what was already known about it prior to the current survey.

Preparing to Write the Review

A literature review should refer mainly to research articles published in journals. For each article, prepare a note card with an identifier (such as the last name of the first author) and notes on relevant aspects of the study. Then, try sorting the cards into groups. Depending on the topic, there can be more than one effective way to group them and some studies might fall into different sets of groups, so try grouping and then regrouping, making multiple cards for individual studies when needed. For instance, here are some ways they might be grouped:

✓ Form one group for each type of finding. For instance, these might be the groupings: (1) studies reporting that Population A is higher than Population B, (2) studies reporting that Population B is higher than Population A, and (3) studies with indeterminate outcomes.

✓ If the research purpose has two variables, three groups might be formed: (1) studies dealing only with the first variable, (2) studies dealing only with the second variable, and (3) studies dealing with both variables.

✓ If the research purpose has two populations, three groups might be formed: (1) studies dealing with Population A, (2) studies dealing with Population B, and (3) studies dealing with both populations.

✓ The studies that are theoretically based might be put in one group and nontheoretical studies might be put in a second group.

✓ The studies that are stronger might be put in one group (e.g., studies using large, representative samples) and those that are weaker put in the other.

There are two purposes for grouping and then regrouping the same set of articles. First, the process will help in getting an overview of the literature that has been collected. For instance, it will help in identifying which groups contain a preponderance of studies, as well as gaps in the literature (e.g., perhaps no articles deal with one of the populations of interest). Second, one or more of the groupings might serve as the basis for the organization of the literature review. For instance, studies dealing only with Variable A might be discussed in one section of the literature review, while studies dealing only with Variable B might be discussed in a later section of the review.

Beginning the Review

While there are many acceptable ways to begin a literature review, two relatively easy and effective ways to begin are described below.

Begin with a Definition

One possibility is to select a key variable and begin the review with its definition. For instance, the authors of Example 5.1 paraphrased a definition based on material reported in three references. Note that each reference in the example is cited in the author-year style (last names of authors and year of publication), which is the style used by the American Psychological Association.

Example 5.1

A definition paraphrased from the literature (for the beginning of a literature review):[1]

Bullying is the unprovoked physical or psychological abuse of an individual by one student or a group of students over time to create an ongoing pattern of harassment and abuse (Batsche & Knoff, 1994; Hoover, Oliver, & Thomson, 1993; Olweus, 1991).

In addition to paraphrasing, it is acceptable to quote a definition offered in the literature. When this is done, it should be introduced in the words of the writer of the current review, as illustrated in Example 5.2.

Example 5.2

A quoted definition introduced with a phrase (for the beginning of a literature review):[2]

Corporal punishment has been defined as "the use of physical force with the intention of causing a child to experience pain, but not injury, for the purpose of correction or control of the child's behavior" (Straus, 1994, p. 4).

If the definitions offered by various writers are not completely compatible, paraphrase or quote them and indicate which one will be used as the definition in the literature review.

---

[1] Whitted, K. S., & Dupper, D. R. (2005). Best practices for preventing or reducing bullying in schools. *Children & Schools, 27,* 167–174.
[2] Modified from Owen, S. S. (2005). The relationship between social capital and corporal punishment in schools: A theoretical inquiry. *Youth & Society, 37,* 85–112.

Begin with Statistics on Incidence Rate or Prevalence

Another way to begin a literature review is to name the problem area and cite some statistics to indicate its incidence or prevalence. Starting with statistics of this type helps to establish the importance of the problem by showing how widespread it is. Example 5.3 illustrates how this was done at the beginning of a literature review.

Example 5.3

Statistics cited on the prevalence of a problem (for the beginning of a literature review):[3]

Adolescents are the most victimized age group in the United States (Snyder & Sickmund, 1999), experiencing violent victimization at a rate nearly 3 times higher than adults (Hashima & Finkelhor, 1999). Research has found that typically about 30% to 50% of adolescents experience some type of victimization in a year (Esbensen & Huizinga, 1991…).

Statistical information on the incidence or prevalence of a problem can often be found cited in research written by others. In addition, a vast array of statistical information gathered by more than 100 federal agencies can be easily located at www.fedstats.gov.

Creating a Synthesis

An effective literature review is more than just a string of summaries of previous studies. Instead, it is a critical synthesis of the literature on the topic. The following suggestions will aid in creating a synthesis.

Discuss Studies in Groups

If several studies have similar findings, discuss them in groups. For instance, in Example 5.4, the writers cite two studies to support one finding.

Example 5.4

Two references cited for one finding (grouping two studies together):[4]

Previous research has established a fairly general socioeconomic risk profile for partner violence. Perhaps the most consistent finding is that women in low-income families are at elevated risk of victimization (Bachman & Saltzman, 1995; Cunradi, Caetano, & Schafer, 2002).

---

[3] Christiansen, E. J., & Evans, W. P. (2005). Adolescent victimization: Testing models of resiliency by gender. *Journal of Early Adolescence, 25,* 298–316.
[4] Frias, S. M., & Angel, R. J. (2005). The risk of partner violence among low-income Hispanic subgroups. *Journal of Marriage and Family, 67,* 552–564.

Be Concise and Provide Details Sparingly

A literature review should be concise. Only studies judged to be especially important should be described in any detail, and typically the details should be provided in only one or two paragraphs. An effective technique is to cite a common finding in a group of studies and then describe the study judged to be most important in more detail than the others. The criteria for determining which studies deserve to be described in more detail than others can vary. An important one is the methodological strengths of the studies. For instance, a previous study with a large, diverse sample might be judged to be more important than others using small, local samples.

When discussing important studies in more detail than the others, it can be helpful to explicitly point out that they are important. This is done in Example 5.5, where the writers refer to a study as a "major study."

Example 5.5

Pointing out that a study being cited is important [bold added for emphasis]:[5]

In a second **major study**, Piquero, Brame, Mazerolle, and Haapanen (2002) followed a group of serious delinquents who were released from the California Youth Authority between 1965 and 1984. Following juvenile parolees 7 years after their release, Piquero and colleagues found a norm of persistence following institutionalization and escalation instead of decline in the immediate transition to young adulthood. In short, they revealed that a substantial proportion of the parolees continued to offend, some very frequently and for violent offenses....

Point Out Trends in the Literature

Help readers get an overview of trends in the literature by explicitly pointing them out. The authors of Example 5.6 have done this.

Example 5.6

Pointing out a trend in the literature:[6]

It is clear that prejudice against different types of romantic relationships exists. A review of past and present public opinion results reveals that nontraditional relationships (e.g., same-sex relationships, younger women dating older men, interracial relationships) have been and continue to be viewed more negatively by society than traditional relationships.... For instance, a 1972 Gallup poll revealed that.... For example, a 1991 poll indicated that....

---

[5] Trulson, C. R., Marquart, J. W., Mullings, J. L., & Caeti, T. J. (2005). In between adolescence and adulthood: Recidivism outcomes of a cohort of state delinquents. *Youth Violence and Juvenile Justice, 3*, 355–387.

[6] Lehmiller, J. J., & Agnew, C. R. (2006). Marginalized relationships: The impact of social disapproval on romantic relationship commitment. *Personality and Social Psychology Bulletin, 32*, 40–51.

Point Out Gaps in the Literature

By grouping and regrouping note cards for the research articles (as discussed at the beginning of this chapter), gaps in the literature may become evident. For instance, it may become evident that certain populations have not been studied or that only a few studies have been conducted on a particular aspect of the research problem. Example 5.7 illustrates how a gap might be pointed out.

Example 5.7

Pointing out a gap in the literature:[7]

A search of the literature revealed that no researchers have examined changes over time in the reporting of domestic assault. It may be that rates of reporting have increased because....

Pointing out a gap in the literature can be especially important if the term-project survey will be helping to fill the gap. Filling a gap in knowledge of a problem may serve as an important justification for conducting the term-project survey.

When asserting that there is a gap, keep in mind that a search of the literature (see Chapter 4) may have failed to identify one or more studies that have, indeed, filled the gap. This may happen because some relevant descriptors were not used in the search or because some relevant studies were not included in the database that was consulted. Thus, it is a good idea to keep careful track of the databases that were consulted and the descriptors used in the search of each one. The databases and the descriptors could be named in the text of the literature review or in a footnote. In other words, it is a good idea to make a qualified assertion such as "Using XXX, YYY, and ZZZ as descriptors in a search of the AAA database, no studies on this topic were found."

Discuss Studies Critically

When studies are cited uncritically in a literature review, readers will assume that they were conducted using reasonably sound methodology. When this is not the case, tip off readers with an indication of the weaknesses. Examples 5.8 and 5.9 do this.

Example 5.8

Critical discussion of previous studies:

The finding that Population A has more favorable attitudes than Population B has been reported in only two studies, each of which employed small, localized samples (Smith 2005; Jones 2006).

---

[7] Modified from Felson, R. B., & Paré, P.-P. (2005). The reporting of domestic violence and sexual assault by nonstrangers to the police. *Journal of Marriage and Family, 67,* 597–610.

Example 5.9

Critical discussion of a previous study:

While Doe's (2006) survey provides an intriguing explanation for this phenomenon, it is important to note that the results are based on a small sample of psychology students who volunteered to participate in the study in exchange for course credit.

It is not necessary to critique each study that is cited in a literature review. However, if a particular study or set of studies is crucial to important points being made in the review, some indication of major weaknesses, if any, should be made.

Use Appropriate Terms to Describe Research Results

All researchers work within limitations. Often, they cannot obtain adequate samples from a population (see Chapter 6 for issues in sampling), and the instruments they use for measurement are subject to various kinds of errors (see Chapters 7 and 8 for issues in instrumentation). As a result, it is not appropriate to use definitive terms such as "prove." Instead, terms that indicate varying degrees of confidence when citing previous research should be used. Box 5A provides a sample of terms that are appropriate under various circumstances. Obviously, for instance, "offer some evidence" indicates less confidence than "strong reason to believe."

Box 5A   *Terms [in bold] that indicate varying degrees of confidence in studies being cited in a literature review (alternatives to "prove").*

1. The results of this pilot study **offer some evidence** that individuals....

2. Evidence from recent surveys **suggests** that individuals....

3. Based on these findings, there is **strong reason to believe** that individuals....

4. Authors of both studies **reported preliminary data suggesting** that individuals....

5. These five recent surveys **provide strong evidence** that individuals....

6. Based on the results, the researchers **reached the tentative conclusion** that individuals....

7. These three surveys **clearly indicate** that individuals....

Provide a Summary

Providing a brief summary of the literature review is an effective way to end it. It helps readers who may have gotten lost in the details get a broad overview of the main findings reported in the review.

Preparing a Reference List

A reference list for the literature review should be provided at the end of a research proposal or research report. Attention to detail is important because errors in content and formatting of a reference list might cause a grade to be lowered for the entire term project. Example 5.10 shows a brief reference list in the style specified in the *Publication Manual of the American Psychological Association*, which is the dominant style manual in the social and behavioral sciences. Note that they are in alphabetical order by surnames. Also note details such as the placement of commas, capitalization (or the lack of), and italics.

Example 5.10
Sample reference list in APA format:

References

Dickens, G., Stubbs, J., Popham, R., & Haw, C. (2005). Smoking in a forensic psychiatric service: A survey of inpatients' views. *Journal of Psychiatric and Mental Health Nursing, 12,* 672–678.

Evans, W. D., Crankshaw, E., Nimsch, C., Morgan-Lopez, A., Farrelly, M. C., & Allen, J. (2006). Media and secondhand smoke exposure: Results from a national survey. *American Journal of Health Behavior, 30,* 62–71.

Gillum, R. F. (2005). Frequency of attendance at religious services and cigarette smoking in American women and men: The Third National Health and Nutrition Examination Survey. *Preventive Medicine: An International Journal Devoted to Practice and Theory, 41,* 607–613.

Oncken, C., McKee, S., Krishnan-Sarin, S., O'Malley, S., & Mazure, C. M. (2005). Knowledge and perceived risk of smoking-related conditions: A survey of cigarette smokers. *Preventive Medicine: An International Journal Devoted to Practice and Theory, 40,* 779–784.

Exercise for Chapter 5

Directions: After you have conducted a search using an electronic database to search for research reports in journals, answer the following questions.

1. In preparation for writing the review, did you try grouping and regrouping note cards for individual studies as suggested at the beginning of this chapter? What types of groupings did you use? Was it helpful? Explain.

2. Did you locate definitions of key terms? If yes, will you paraphrase them in your literature review? Will you quote them?

3. Have you located statistics on the prevalence and incidence for inclusion in your literature review? If yes, will you use them at the beginning of your review?

4. Are there any clear trends in the findings of the research you will be citing in your review? Explain.

5. Have you identified any gaps that you plan to mention in your review? Explain.

6. Are some of the studies you will cite clearly weak (e.g., small samples)? Will you point out such weaknesses in your review?

7. Do some of the studies you plan to cite provide stronger evidence than others? Will you use appropriate verbs to distinguish between them? If yes, give some examples.

8. Will your reference list be in APA format? If so, select one of the studies you will cite and write the reference in APA style here and have it reviewed for correctness of formatting by a fellow student.

Chapter 6

Selecting a Sample

This chapter covers the basics of sampling as well as some practical advice for students conducting a term-project survey on a short timeline with limited resources.

Sampling Basics

A survey researcher should identify a population of interest. The population might be small, such as all graduate students majoring in sociology at a university, or it might be large, such as all undergraduates majoring in sociology in the United States.

If a population is small and accessible, it may be possible to use all members of the population as participants in a survey, negating the need to sample. For large populations, it is more efficient to sample than to survey all members.

Ideally, a sample should be both unbiased and large enough to yield reliable results. By definition, a random sample is an unbiased sample.

Simple Random Sampling

Simple random sampling provides every member of a population with an equal chance of being selected. One way to draw a simple random sample is to put the names of all members of a population on slips of paper, put the slips in a hat, mix them up, and draw out the number needed for the survey. A more efficient method is to use a set of random numbers. A set of random numbers is a set in which the numbers have no sequence and no relationship to each other. To understand what this means, suppose a researcher put the ten single digits from 0 to 9 on slips of paper, mixed them up in a hat, pulled out one, and wrote it down. Then the researcher put the slip back into the hat, mixed them again, and drew out another one, and wrote it down next to the first number drawn. Continuing this process, the researcher would create a set of random numbers (i.e., each number has no relationship to any other number).

Fortunately, the process of creating a set of random numbers can be simplified by using a random number generator on the Internet. Searching for "random number generator" using a search engine such as Google, a number of free Internet sites that generate random lists of numbers can be located. Examples 6.1 and 6.2 on the next page illustrate the use of two free Internet sites to select simple random samples.[1]

---

[1] Internet sites sometimes cease to exist. If the ones in Examples 6.1 and 6.2 no longer exist at the addresses given in the examples, other similar sites can be found using a search engine, such as Google.

Example 6.1

Using random numbers generated at www.random.org:

A researcher had a population of 200 and wanted to draw a sample of 25. First, she numbered the 200 individuals in the population from 1 to 200. Then, she went online to www.random.org, which has three columns on the home page. Under the middle column labeled "How?" the researcher clicked on the link for "randomized sequences," which brought up a page with dialog boxes. In the box for the "smallest value," she typed the number 1, and in the box for the "largest value," she typed the number 200. Then, she typed on the link for "generate sequence" and obtained a list of 200 numbers in random order. Since the sample size was to be 25, she used the first 25 numbers in the list to identify individuals for the sample. These are the numbers that were generated: 71, 112, 135, 47, 195, 187, 9, 17, 196, 43, 127, 51, 167, 86, 160, 128, 24, 154, 82, 105, 122, 53, 31, 182, 113.[2]

Example 6.2

Using random numbers generated at www.randomizer.org/form.htm:

A researcher had a population of 200 and wanted to draw a sample of 25. First, he numbered the 200 individuals in the population from 1 to 200. Then he went online to www.randomizer.org/form.htm, and changed only the following two defaults: (a) he changed the "5" to "25" to the right of the question "How many members per set?" and (b) he changed "50" to "200" to the right of "Number range." Then he clicked on the link for "Randomize Now" and obtained these 25 random numbers: 196, 176, 115, 32, 10, 182, 120, 42, 88, 47, 177, 181, 135, 190, 111, 83, 171, 136, 121, 62, 173, 151, 150, 188, and 11, which are the number-names of the 25 individuals selected for the sample.

Stratified Random Sampling

In stratified random sampling, the population is first divided into subgroups (i.e., strata), and then a simple random sample is drawn from each subgroup. Consider Example 6.3, in which the subgroups are men and women.

Example 6.3

Drawing a stratified random sample:

A team of researchers was conducting a survey on job satisfaction among college professors at a university. The population consisted of 80 women and 120 men. The researchers realized that using simple random sampling, by the luck of the draw, might yield a sample with disproportionate numbers of men and women. To prevent this from happening, they employed stratified random sampling, using gender as the

---

[2] Note that each time the random number generator is used, a different set of random numbers will be generated. For instance in Example 6.1, the first three numbers are 71, 112, and 135. On a second use of the same generator, the first three numbers were 4, 89, 131.

stratification variable. Specifically, they treated the women and men as separate populations, and drew a simple random sample of 20% of the women and 20% of the men. This yielded a total sample consisting of 16 women and 24 men. Thus, the sample was representative of the population in terms of its gender composition.

For stratification to be effective, the stratification variable must have some bearing on the variables being measured in the survey. For instance, for a survey on job satisfaction among college professors, stratification on the basis of eye color (a variable that is probably irrelevant to the variable of job satisfaction) would not produce a superior sample to a simple random sample drawn from the entire population without stratification.

Random Cluster Sampling

A "cluster" is defined as a pre-existing group. Some populations are naturally divided into clusters. For instance, each class section on a college campus is a cluster. To draw a random cluster sample, first number each cluster, and then draw a simple random sample of the clusters, using the procedures for simple random sampling described near the beginning of this chapter.

When the clusters are heterogeneous, a large number of clusters should be drawn. For instance, the clusters of class sections on a college campus are heterogeneous in many important respects, such as age (students in freshman English tend to be younger than students in graduate-level classes), major field of study, part-time versus full-time status (evening and weekend sections may have more part-time students), and so on. If only a small number of class sections were drawn from such a heterogeneous population, the resulting sample might be seriously unrepresentative. For instance, drawing only three class sections from a college campus (even if each section has 30 students, for a total of 90) probably would not provide an optimal amount of diversity if, for instance, two of the three class sections happened, at random, to be freshman English classes.

In contrast, when the clusters are relatively homogeneous, an adequate sample can be drawn using a relatively small number of clusters. For instance, if the population consists of only freshmen, drawing a small number of class sections of a required course for freshmen might be deemed to be adequate.

Systematic Sampling

A systematic sample can be obtained by selecting every n^{th} individual. For instance, if n is set by a researcher to be "3," the researcher would draw every third person from a class roster to obtain a systematic sample.

While systematic sampling is usually done from a list of the population, a variation on it can be used when identifying individuals in public places as potential participants in a survey. Example 6.4 shows how one team of researchers did this using $n = 10$.

Example 6.4

Systematically sampling individuals in a public place:[3]

Participants were recruited from two types of venues: dance clubs and social settings (campus "hangouts" and coffee shops) in NYC.... Once the venues were selected, field staff would offer participation to every 10th person to cross a predetermined threshold (either a point on the line to get into a dance club, or a place just inside the main entrance for some venues).

For technical reasons, systematic sampling is not equivalent to random sampling. Nevertheless, for all practical purposes, it is as good as random sampling and greatly superior to convenience sampling (e.g., using individuals who happen to be convenient as participants).

Sample Size

Larger samples yield more precise results (i.e., are less subject to random sampling error) than smaller samples. However, there are diminishing returns as a sample size is increased. For instance, consider a sample consisting of 30 individuals. If an additional 30 individuals were added (for a total sample size of 60), the sample would be greatly improved. Now, consider a sample of 2,000 individuals. Increasing the sample size by an additional 30 (for a total sample size of 2,030) cannot have much of an effect on the results because the potential influence of the additional 30 in such a large sample would be minimal.

Box 6A on the next page shows recommended sample sizes for populations of varying sizes. In the box, N stands for the population size, while n stands for the recommended sample size. For instance, the information in the box shows that for a population of 200, the recommended sample size is 132.

Techniques for Term-Project Samples

For a term project, drawing a sample at random (either simple random, stratified random, or random cluster sampling) or drawing a systematic sample should be done whenever possible. However, even professional researchers often find that they are unable to use these techniques for logistic reasons, so it should not be surprising if students conducting a term project might also find it difficult to do so.

The following are suggested techniques to improve sampling when an "ideal" sample cannot be drawn for a term-project survey.

---

[3] Parsons, J. T., Halkitis, P. N., & Bimbi, D. S. (2006). Club drug use among young adults frequenting dance clubs and other social venues in New York City. *Journal of Child & Adolescent Substance Abuse*, *15*, 1–14.

Consider Adjusting the Research Problem

For a term-project survey, some students might want to adjust the research purpose in light of the accessibility of potential participants. For instance, if a psychology student has access to a good sample of psychology majors (with assistance of the psychology department), a research purpose involving all undergraduates on a campus might be changed to involve only psychology majors.

Box 6A   *Table of recommended sample sizes (n) for populations (N) with finite sizes*[4]

N	n	N	n	N	n
10	10	220	140	1,200	291
15	14	230	144	1,300	297
20	19	240	148	1,400	302
25	24	250	152	1,500	306
30	28	260	155	1,600	310
35	32	270	159	1,700	313
40	36	280	162	1,800	317
45	40	290	165	1,900	320
50	44	300	169	2,000	322
55	48	320	175	2,200	327
60	52	340	181	2,400	331
65	56	360	186	2,600	335
70	59	380	191	2,800	338
75	63	400	196	3,000	341
80	66	420	201	3,500	346
85	70	440	205	4,000	351
90	73	460	210	4,500	354
95	76	480	214	5,000	357
100	80	500	217	6,000	361
110	86	550	226	7,000	364
120	92	600	234	8,000	367
130	97	650	242	9,000	368
140	103	700	248	10,000	370
150	108	750	254	15,000	375
160	113	800	260	20,000	377
170	118	850	265	30,000	379
180	123	900	269	40,000	380
190	127	950	274	50,000	381
200	132	1,000	278	75,000	382
210	136	1,100	285	100,000	384

[4] Adapted from: Krejcie, R. V., & Morgan, D. W. (1970). Determining sample size for research activities. *Educational and Psychological Measurement, 30*, 607–610.

Use Diverse Locations and Times

Suppose that a sample will be obtained by approaching students on campus and asking them to agree to be interviewed for a survey. For such a project, using only one location such as at the campus cafeteria entrance, might unnecessarily bias the sample because students who tend to use the cafeteria might be systematically different from those who do not. Thus, soliciting participation at the entrances to a variety of buildings on campus probably will provide a superior sample to one conducted at only the entrance to the cafeteria.

In addition to striving for diversity in location, a researcher might strive for diversity in times. For instance, seeking participation of only students arriving for morning classes might unnecessarily bias the sample because those who attend morning classes might be systematically different in a variety of ways from students who attend afternoon and evening classes.

Use Population Demographics When Planning the Sample

The office of institutional research on most campuses routinely compiles demographic information (i.e., background information) on the student body, and this information is generally available to the public. This information can be used by students who are trying to draw a representative sample of a student body. For instance, consider a student who will be asking professors for permission to administer questionnaires to students enrolled in their classes. If the office of institutional research indicates that 15% of the students in the population are graduate students, the student can plan to request permission to survey a limited number of graduate-level classes, so that about 15% of the final sample consists of graduate students.

Example 6.5 illustrates another way this technique can be implemented.

Example 6.5

Using population demographics when planning a survey:

A student knows that 60% of the undergraduates on a campus are women, based on population demographics supplied by the office of institutional research. The student plans to interview 30 undergraduates by approaching them at various locations on campus. To have the sample be representative in terms of gender, the student wants 18 (60% of the 30) of the participants to be women and 12 to be men. Thus, the student plans to stop approaching women for interviews once 18 have been obtained; likewise, the student plans to stop approaching men once 12 have been obtained.

Use Population Demographics When Analyzing the Data

Consider a student who used the campus mail (with permission) to solicit students to participate in a survey. After calculating the average age of the respondents, the student compares the average to the average age of the population, as determined by the office of institutional research. Finding that the average age of the respondents is much higher than the average age in the population, the student deletes some of the questionnaires submitted by older respondents, thus making the sample more representative of the population in terms of age.[5]

Track Information on Nonvolunteers

Nonvolunteers are potential participants who were contacted but refused to participate. Consider that a student solicits students at various locations on campus to be interviewed for a survey. Keeping track of the rates of participation at the various locations might reveal, for instance, a higher rate of participation from students entering the cafeteria than from students entering classroom buildings. Even if the influence of this on the results is not clear, this differential in rates of participation should be noted in the research report in order to advise readers of a potential bias in sampling.

For mailed surveys, keeping track of zip codes can shed light on how representative a sample is. For instance, if 30% of the questionnaires were mailed to one of the zip codes but only 20% of the responses were posted in that zip code, the student could report this discrepancy, noting that caution should be used in interpreting the results.[6]

Consider Seeking a Community-Based Sample

In some academic fields, much research is conducted using campus-based samples. When replicating or extending previous research based on campus samples, using a community-based sample could be an important strength. For instance, if a series of studies have been conducted using biased campus samples (e.g., introductory psychology students who volunteer for course credit), a term-project survey using a community-based sample would extend knowledge of the research problem—even if the community-based sample is also biased.

Obviously, community-based samples can be obtained by soliciting participation in public places. In addition, community groups and organizations such as social clubs, religious institutions, and neighborhood councils might provide access to their members, especially if the results have the potential to help the groups and organizations.

Increasingly, researchers are using the Internet to solicit community-based samples. For a term-project survey, e-mail lists might be obtained for little or no charge from professional associations, community organizations, and other groups. In addition, e-mail lists (just as physical mail lists) can be rented from list brokers. Many of these might be out of the financial range of students conducting a term-project survey. However, for students who might want to explore this possibility, list brokers of various types can be identified by using "list broker" and "e-mail list broker" as search terms using a search engine such as Google.

---

[5] When deleting in this example, it is best to identify all respondents over a certain cut-off age and then select at random the ones to be deleted. The obvious disadvantage of deleting responses is that the sample size will be reduced. Students who have more advanced training in statistics may prefer to "weight" the results, giving less weight to the responses of the older participants without deleting any of them.

[6] Note that individuals living in one zip code often differ in important ways (such as income) from those in other zip codes. Techniques for mailed surveys are discussed in Chapter 10.

Emphasize Representativeness over Sample Size

As a general rule, obtaining a representative sample is more important than using a large sample. Thus, if forced to choose, it is usually better to work with a smaller representative sample than a larger biased sample.

Exercise for Chapter 6

1. Do you anticipate using any of the following: simple random sampling, stratified random sampling, random cluster sampling, or systematic sampling? If yes, which one? If no, why not?

2. What is the anticipated sample size for your survey? Get feedback from other students on the anticipated size and write their reactions here.

3. Indicate whether you might be using each of the following techniques. If you will be using any of them, explain how you will implement them.

   A. Adjusting the Research Problem

   B. Using Diverse Locations and Times

   C. Using Population Demographics When Planning the Sample

   D. Using Population Demographics When Analyzing the Data

   E. Tracking Information on Nonvolunteers

   F. Seeking a Community-Based Sample

   G. Emphasizing Representativeness over Sample Size

Chapter 7

Identifying Existing Instruments

In research, the term "instrument" refers to any type of measurement tool such as achievement tests, questionnaires, interview schedules, personality scales, or attitude surveys. This chapter covers the basics of locating existing instruments, while the next chapter shows how to build new instruments, which may be necessary if none of the existing instruments are on target for a particular research purpose.

Unpublished Instruments

The term "unpublished instruments" refers to instruments that are *not* published by test publishers (i.e., publishers who publish tests, usually on a for-profit basis).

Instruments Reproduced in Research Articles

The research articles collected during a search of the literature (see Chapter 4) are often very helpful in identifying unpublished instruments that might be used in a term-project survey.

Researchers who build new instruments for use in their research sometimes include copies of the complete instruments in their research articles. While the complete instruments are sometimes shown in tables in the body of the articles, they are often included in appendices at the end of research articles, so be sure to check for appendices at the end of articles that might contain instruments. Box 7A on the next page shows a portion of an instrument included in a research report. Note that it is not formatted with choices for each item, which is often the case with instruments provided in research articles. To use this instrument, the choices in the Note at the bottom of the box (from "I am very sure" to "I am very unsure") would need to be reprinted under each item, with spaces for participants to indicate their choices.

Box 7B on the next page shows a portion of an instrument that appeared as an appendix at the end of a research article. Notice that in this instrument, "ONE DRINK" is specifically defined within the questionnaire. It is important for instruments to contain definitions of any variables that might be open to interpretation by respondents.

Box 7A *Portion of an unpublished instrument located in a research article.*

Story #1: Imagine that you are hanging out with friends *at a friend's house.* You are having fun. While getting some food, you are offered a cigarette. How sure are you that you could say "no" to the cigarette offer and not smoke:

43. If the person who asked you to smoke was your best friend?

44. If the person who asked you to smoke was an older student who you admired?

45. If it was a group of friends who asked you to smoke?

46. If your best friend called you a coward for not smoking?

47. If an older student who you admired called you a coward for not smoking?

48. If a group of your friends called you a coward for not smoking?

Note. All items were scored on a 4-point Likert scale: (3) I am very sure, (2) I am somewhat sure, (1) I am somewhat unsure, and (0) I am very unsure.

From Langlois, M. A., Petosa, R. L., & Hallam, J. S. (2005). Measuring self-efficacy and outcome expectations for resisting social pressures to smoke. *Journal of Child & Adolescent Substance Abuse, 15,* 1–17. Copyright © 2005 by the Haworth press. Reprinted with permission.

Box 7B *Portion of an unpublished instrument located in an appendix of a research article.*

Quantity–Frequency Measure

1. DURING THE PAST 30 DAYS, on how many days did you have *any* beverage containing alcohol (including beer, wine, or liquor)? _____

For Question 2, any of the following count as ONE DRINK:

      one glass (or one can) of beer or

      one glass (4 ounces) of wine or

      one shot (one ounce) of liquor or other distilled spirits or

      one single-shot mixed drink (a double shot counts as 2 drinks)

2. DURING THE PAST 30 DAYS, on days when you did drink alcohol, how many drinks did you usually have?

          _____DRINKS per drinking day

From Fishburne, J. W., & Brown, J. M. (2006). How do college students estimate their drinking?: Comparing consumption patterns among quantity–frequency, graduated frequency, and timeline follow-back methods. *Journal of Alcohol and Drug Education, 50,* 15–31. Reprinted with permission.

Instruments Mentioned in Research Articles

Researchers often report on the use of unpublished instruments but do not include complete copies of them in their research reports. However, they often provide references that can be helpful. Example 7.1 illustrates that following up on references given for instruments can sometimes lead to copies of the complete instruments.

Example 7.1

Locating an unpublished instrument through a reference:

A student was planning a survey on smoking motivations and found this statement under the subheading Self-Report Measures in a research article: "During the screening session, smokers completed...the Wisconsin Inventory of Smoking Dependence Motives (Piper et al., 2004)."[1] The instrument was not included in the article. However, looking up the Piper et al. 2004 article in the *PsycARTICLES* database, the student found a complete copy of the instrument.[2]

Note that by going to the Piper et al. 2004 article in Example 7.1, the student not only found the complete instrument but also found details of its development as well as extensive information on its reliability and validity, which could be summarized in the student's report on the term-project survey.

Sometimes researchers develop new, unpublished instruments for which there are no references and do not include complete copies of the instruments in the research articles in which they are mentioned. In cases such as these, the author of the research article may be contacted. Almost all journals provide contact information (including e-mail addresses) for the authors, either on the first page of journal articles or following the references. Requests for copies for use in term-project surveys are often honored.

Databases of Unpublished Instruments

There are several major databases of unpublished instruments that can be consulted to locate instruments relevant to a research problem for a term-project survey. Box 7C briefly describes three major ones, and Box 7D shows partial output from one of them. Consult with a reference librarian on the availability of these and others that might be available through the campus library.

---

[1] This statement was found in Piper, M. E., & Curtin, J. J. (2006). Tobacco withdrawal and negative affect: An analysis of initial emotional response intensity and voluntary emotion regulation. *Journal of Abnormal Psychology, 115*, 96–102.

[2] The reference that contains the complete instrument is: Piper, M., Federman, E., Piasecki, T., Bolt, D., Smith, S., Fiore, M., & Baker, T. (2004). A multiple motives approach to tobacco dependence: The Wisconsin Inventory of Smoking Dependence Motives. *Journal of Consulting and Clinical Psychology, 72*, 139–154.

Box 7C   *Major databases for locating unpublished instruments.*

ETS Test Collection

This database contains information on more than 10,000 instruments. Access to the database is free via the Internet at www.ets.org/testcoll/. Box 7D shows the results of a search using the term "alcohol." The titles of the 10 instruments shown in the box are links. Clicking on each title provides more information, including the availability of the instruments. Often, they are available through journal articles for which references are given. Sometimes, addresses to individuals or organizations are given for obtaining copies. In other instances, they are available for purchase at a nominal charge from ETS (Educational Testing Service) via the Internet.

Directory of Unpublished Experimental Measures

Published in volumes over time, the current volume indexes more than 1,700 unpublished instruments that were gathered from journals in the social and behavioral sciences. In addition to descriptions of the instruments, information on their availability is provided. Major college libraries have copies of the volumes in this series, which are also available for purchase via www.apa.org.

Health and Psychosocial Instruments (HaPI)

With an emphasis on instruments in nursing and medicine, this database also includes a wide variety of instruments in related fields such as psychology and social work. It includes references to journal articles where more information on instruments can be found. Published by Ovid Technologies, Inc., this database is available through large academic libraries.

Box 7D   *Instruments identified through a search of the ETS Test Collection Database using the search term "alcohol."*

Title	Year	Abstract
Adolescent Alcohol Involvement Scale (AAIS).	1979	The Adolescent Alcohol Involvement Scale (AAIS) is designed to identify adolescents who are misusing alcohol. The AAIS was primarily designed as a research tool, and was not designed to diagnose alcoholism in adolescents. It consists of 14 questions in simple language to be used as a self-report. Reliability and validity are discussed. (JW)
Alcohol Abstinence Self-Efficacy Scale.	1994	The Alcohol Abstinence Self-Efficacy Scale (AASE) was designed to measure problem drinkers' evaluations of their perceived temptation to drink and their efficacy to abstain in 20 common situations. It consists of 40 statements rated on a 5-point, Likert-type scale. It takes about 10 minutes to complete and has 4 scales: negative affect, social positive, physical and other concerns, and withdrawal and urges. It may be used for outcome evaluation and program evaluation where the goal of intervention is abstinence. Reliability and validity are discussed.
Alcohol Assessment and Treatment Profile.	1984	This instrument is designed to assess an individual's pattern of drinking, and the ways in which a treatment can be instituted. Background data and history of the person's drinking patterns are collected. Self-Concept and interpersonal relations are regarded by the clinician to get a better assessment in treating each patient. A termination summary is initiated, which includes the presenting problem, intervention goals, personality assessment, treatment, and outcome.
Alcohol Assessment Interview; Psychosocial Interview Guide.	1963	Structured interview used to distinguish between alcoholics and nonalcoholics. Used to determine level of severity of alcoholism. Available as entry 3.1.
Alcohol Attitude Questionnaire.	1970	Used in a study of college students to examine their attitudes toward drinking and their drinking behavior. Can be used in additional studies to determine if there are changes in drinking trends. Includes questions on demographic data, also.
Alcohol Awareness Test.	1980	Designed to assess knowledge of alcohol and its use. Instrument may serve as basis for providing insight into the nature and effects of alcohol through discussion of correct responses.
Alcohol Behavior, Attitude, and Awareness Inventory.	1987	This inventory is designed to assess drinking and driving behaviors and attitudes, community resources awareness and traits associated with adult children of alcoholics. It is used with students entering a health education class in which drinking and driving issues will be part of the curriculum. It can be used as a needs assessment, baseline data gathering instrument, and a formative, process, and summative evaluation tool. Information on validity and reliability studies with college students is included. Items are presented as forced choice or in multiple choice format. The items are written at a seventh grade reading level. Eight factors were identified, including general alcohol experiences, personal expectation, abusive drinking behaviors, interpersonal behaviors, law-related attitudes toward drinking and driving, family problems with alcohol, "cavalierness," and individual community resource awareness.
Alcohol Clinical Index: Strategies for Identifying Patients with Alcohol Problems.	1987	[No abstract available.]
Alcohol Dependence Scale.	1984	Provides a brief measure of the extent to which the use of alcohol has progressed from psychological involvement to impaired control. Designed to provide a brief but psychometrically sound measure of the alcohol dependence syndrome, to be used as both a research and clinical diagnostic tool. May be administered in either a questionnaire or interview format.
Alcohol Effects on Self and Others.	1987	[No abstract available.]

Published Instruments

The term "published instruments" refers to instruments that are published by test publishers (i.e., publishers who sell tests).

An advantage of published instruments is that they have usually undergone more extensive development work than unpublished instruments, including studies of their reliability and validity.

There are two disadvantages to published tests. First, test publishers naturally emphasize instruments that have the potential for widespread use in diagnosis and screening, mainly in psychology and education. As such, published instruments are less likely to be suitable for use in specialized term-project surveys than unpublished instruments. Second, fees must be paid to purchase or rent and use published instruments, which may be beyond the financial reach of students conducting term-project surveys. Nevertheless, some students may find suitable published tests for use in their projects by consulting the databases described in Box 7E.

Box 7E   *Major databases for locating published instruments.*

Tests in Print

The purpose of this database is to index all tests in the social and behavioral sciences, including education, that are commercially available for purchase. Contact information for test publishers is provided. Published by The Buros Institute for Mental Measurements, this index is available in most academic libraries.

Mental Measurements Yearbook

Contains critical reviews of selected commercially available tests. The yearbook covers only a limited number of available tests. Published by The Buros Institute for Mental Measurements, this yearbook is available in most academic libraries.

Tests

Similar in purpose to *Tests in Print* (see above), this is an index with information on tests in psychology, education, and business. Published by Pro-Ed, Inc., this index is available in most academic libraries.

Test Critiques

Similar in purpose to the *Mental Measurements Yearbook* (see above), this database contains extensive information on and reviews of a variety of published tests. Published by Pro-Ed, Inc., this index is available in most academic libraries.

Issues in Test Reliability and Validity

Ideally, students who conduct term-project research will want to use instruments that are both highly reliable and valid. For both unpublished and published instruments, information on these characteristics is often available. For instance, in a research article in which a new instrument is described, preliminary evidence on reliability and validity may be reported. For published instruments, publishers usually provide manuals that contain extensive information on these topics.

When writing a research proposal and research report, the available information on reliability and validity should be briefly summarized. While it is beyond the scope of this book to provide detailed information on techniques for estimating reliability and validity, Appendix B provides an overview of them.

Obtaining Permission to Use Existing Instruments

Research articles in journals are copyrighted, usually by publishers of the journals. Students using instruments found in journal articles are obligated to contact the copyright holders to obtain written permission to reproduce the instruments for use in their term projects. Likewise, published tests are copyrighted. Purchasing published instruments almost always allows restricted use of (but not the right to duplicate) the instruments.

If the author of an unpublished instrument provides a copy for a student to use in his or her project, the student should also seek written permission to duplicate and use it.

Exercise for Chapter 7

Directions: Share your answers to this exercise with other students who may still be trying to identify a topic for their term projects.

1. When searching the literature on your research topic, did you find any complete instruments (reproduced in the articles) that you might use in your term-project survey? Explain.

2. When searching the literature on your research topic, did you find any mention of unpublished instruments (without complete copies) that you might use in your term-project survey? If yes, were there references that might help in locating complete copies? Will you be contacting the authors of the research articles to solicit complete copies? Explain.

3. Have you consulted any of the databases for locating unpublished instruments listed in Box 7C? If yes, were they helpful? Explain.

4. Have you consulted any of the databases for locating published instruments listed in Box 7D? If yes, were they helpful? Explain.

5. Before reading Appendix A, how familiar were you with the concepts of reliability and validity? To what extent was the material in Appendix B helpful in increasing your understanding of these concepts?

6. If you will be using a copyrighted instrument, what steps will you take to seek permission to use it in your term-project survey?

7. At this point, do you plan to use an existing instrument or to construct your own new instrument (a possibility discussed in the next chapter)?

Chapter 8
Constructing Instruments

Frequently, students are unable to find existing instruments that are suitable for their specific research problems and need to construct their own instruments.[1] This chapter covers the basics for constructing these types of instruments: (a) attitude scales, (b) tests of knowledge, (c) questionnaires on programs and services, (d) questionnaires on self-reported behaviors, and (e) interview schedules.

Constructing Attitude Scales

An attitude is a general orientation toward an entity such as a group, type of person, organization, and so on. It consists of *feelings* that have the potential to lead to *actions*. Thus, to measure attitudes, questions about both feelings (e.g., feelings about going to school in the mornings), and actions or potential actions (e.g., faking illness in order to be excused from school) are often asked.

Planning an Attitude Scale

To plan an attitude scale, first identify the broad components of the object of the attitudes. For instance, for attitudes toward math, the components might be (a) perceived usefulness of math in everyday activities, (b) perceived usefulness of math in academic activities, (c) enjoyment of math courses, (d) desire to learn more about math, and so on. The plan should specify how many attitude scale items will be written for each component such as "five items asking about enjoyment of math classes," "desire to learn more about math," and so on.

The broad components listed as the basis for an attitude scale can be used in a developmental study with a small number of individuals. For instance, individuals could be asked, "What is the first thing that comes to mind when you think about the last math class you took?" and "How important is math to you in everyday life? Explain." Answers to questions like these can help in identifying specific characteristics to ask about in items in the attitude-toward-math scale.

Writing an Attitude Scale

While numerous approaches to the measurement of attitudes have been proposed and studied, the approach suggested by Rensis Likert in the 1930s has been found to be about as good as or better than the others for most research purposes. The basic concept of a Likert

---

[1] Depending on their course objectives, some instructors may require students to construct their own instruments, even if existing ones are available for their research purposes.

scale is simple: Write straightforward statements about the object of the attitude and provide choices that vary from Strongly Agree to Strongly Disagree.

Each statement in a Likert scale should deal with only one point. Otherwise, participants will find themselves in the untenable position of answering what are, in effect, two or more questions with only one set of choices. For instance, the first item in Example 8.1 asks about two elements. Each should be asked about separately as illustrated in the improved version in Example 8.1.

Example 8.1

A Likert statement asking about two points (not recommended):

The new Medicare changes are expensive and a waste of government money.
   ☐ Strongly Agree   ☐ Agree   ☐ Neutral   ☐ Disagree   ☐ Strongly Disagree

Improved version, with one item on each point (recommended):

The new Medicare changes are expensive.
   ☐ Strongly Agree   ☐ Agree   ☐ Neutral   ☐ Disagree   ☐ Strongly Disagree
The new Medicare changes are a waste of government money.
   ☐ Strongly Agree   ☐ Agree   ☐ Neutral   ☐ Disagree   ☐ Strongly Disagree

If all of the statements in a Likert-type instrument reflect favorable attitudes, some respondents may move quickly through them, answering them based on their overall attitude and not consider the content of each item carefully. To overcome this problem, about half should be favorable and half should be unfavorable. Note that an unfavorable statement can be made by using the word "not" as in this statement: "Math is not my favorite subject in school." However, research on the use of negatives such as "not" indicate that they can be confusing to some respondents, so they should be avoided. Example 8.2 shows a statement that expresses an unfavorable sentiment without the use of the word "not."

Example 8.2

A Likert statement expressing an unfavorable sentiment without the use of "not" (recommended):

Math is my least favorite subject in school.
   ☐ Strongly Agree   ☐ Agree   ☐ Neutral   ☐ Disagree   ☐ Strongly Disagree

Reverse scoring should be used for the items expressing unfavorable sentiments. Thus, if Strongly Agree is given 5 points, Agree is given 4 points, and so on for a favorable statement, the reverse should be done for unfavorable ones (i.e., Strongly Disagree is given 5 points, Disagree is given 4 points, and so on). Having done this, the total number of points for each respondent can be counted up, resulting in an overall attitude score.

Sometimes it is necessary to ask about hypothetical experiences. For example, suppose you wanted to measure attitudes toward people who are HIV+. If it is likely that many of your respondents do not personally know anyone who is HIV+, you may wish to establish a hypothetical situation and ask respondents how they would feel and act in response. Example 8.3 illustrates this technique.

Example 8.3[2]

An attitude scale based on a hypothetical situation:

Directions: Suppose a new classmate told you that he or she is HIV+. Answer the following questions about your reactions.

1. I would avoid spending time with the person.
   ☐ Strongly Agree   ☐ Agree   ☐ Disagree   ☐ Strongly Disagree

2. I would treat the person just as I would anyone else.
   ☐ Strongly Agree   ☐ Agree   ☐ Disagree   ☐ Strongly Disagree

3. I would stay away from club meetings if that person joined the club.
   ☐ Strongly Agree   ☐ Agree   ☐ Disagree   ☐ Strongly Disagree

4. I would consider becoming friends with the person.
   ☐ Strongly Agree   ☐ Agree   ☐ Disagree   ☐ Strongly Disagree

5. I would ask to be transferred to another class.
   ☐ Strongly Agree   ☐ Agree   ☐ Disagree   ☐ Strongly Disagree

6. I would find it difficult to concentrate on my schoolwork with the person in the classroom.
   ☐ Strongly Agree   ☐ Agree   ☐ Disagree   ☐ Strongly Disagree

7. I would welcome the person to the class.
   ☐ Strongly Agree   ☐ Agree   ☐ Disagree   ☐ Strongly Disagree

8. I would be afraid of getting HIV.
   ☐ Strongly Agree   ☐ Agree   ☐ Disagree   ☐ Strongly Disagree

9. I would feel comfortable playing on a sports team with the person.
   ☐ Strongly Agree   ☐ Agree   ☐ Disagree   ☐ Strongly Disagree

Pilot Testing an Attitude Scale

After the attitude scale items have been written and reviewed by others, the scale should be pilot tested. The pilot test should be conducted with respondents who will not be included in the main study. To get information on the quality of the items, two techniques can be used. First, the "think aloud" technique can be employed by asking each respondent in the pilot study to read each statement aloud and state what they are thinking as they answer each

---

[2] The term "HIV+" should be defined in the directions unless the item writer believes that all respondents are familiar with the term. For example, if the attitude scale is being administered to students who just completed a comprehensive unit on HIV/AIDS, it may not be necessary to define it.

one. When doing this, it is not uncommon to find that some respondents attach different interpretations to certain items than the author did when writing them. This often leads to rewriting some items to make them clearer. The second technique is to ask respondents in the pilot study to write notes in the margins on anything that bothers them, is unclear, and so on.

Constructing Tests of Knowledge

For measuring knowledge in a survey, most researchers rely heavily on test items that can be objectively scored. For measuring knowledge in a survey, a popular form is the multiple-choice item. However, there may be less resistance to participation if the true–false form is used because true–false items are easier to read and respond to than multiple-choice items.

Planning a Test of Knowledge

The key to successful planning of a test of knowledge is to base the test on a list of objectives. Each objective should name a fact or understanding that an individual who is knowledgeable should know. For instance, to plan a test on knowledge of safe food-handling practices in the kitchen, authoritative sources (such as government publications) could be gathered and a list of objectives prepared based on them.

In the planning stage, decisions should be made regarding whether the test will cover all the objectives or just a sample of them. As a general rule, if there are 12 or fewer objectives, all of them should be covered in the test. With a larger number of objectives, those deemed less important than others might be omitted from the plan in order to keep the test reasonably short.

Have the plan reviewed, asking the reviewers to comment on the adequacy of the coverage of the objectives.

Writing Multiple-Choice Items

A multiple-choice item should have one choice that is correct and two or more *distracters* (i.e., plausible incorrect choices). Plausible distracters are choices that might appeal to unskilled or unknowledgeable examinees. It is easiest to understand the concept of plausible distracters by considering a math item. Example 8.4 shows a multiple-choice item with its correct choice as well as two distracters, with the rationale as to why the distracters might be plausible stated in small print.

Example 8.4

Multiple choice items with plausible distracters:

Fifty-seven people will be attending a charity event. Each person will bring three toys to be donated to the charity. What is the total number of toys that will be brought?

A. 171 (correct choice: $57 \times 3 = 171$)

B. 151 (distracter: Incorrect answer obtained by failing to carry the "2" in multiplication)

C. 60 (distracter: Incorrect choice obtained by summing 57 and 3)

An ambiguity in a multiple-choice item can cause skilled examinees to make errors. These are often hard for item writers to spot because an item writer may have one mental set, while some examinees might have another. Consider the multiple-choice item in Example 8.5. What is the ambiguity?[3]

Example 8.5

An ambiguous multiple-choice item:

What is the largest state east of the Mississippi River?

A. New York

B. Pennsylvania

C. Georgia

D. Virginia

The items should be reviewed by others and revised, if necessary.

Writing True–False Items

A true–false item should contain a statement covering only one point, and the statement should be unequivocally right or wrong. The first true–false item in Example 8.6 on the next page shows a single true–false item that covers two points. It also shows the improved version (on the next page) with two items, each covering a single point. Note that one of the points is true (the last major reform was under the Clinton administration) while the second point is false (welfare does *not* provide benefits mainly for racial minorities).

---

[3] The ambiguity stems from the fact that "largest" might refer to population (in which case, the answer is New York) or to geographical size (in which case, the answer is Georgia). Note that the distracters are plausible because they all name states that are relatively large (in both senses), and they all are located east of the Mississippi River.

Example 8.6

A true–false item covering two points (not recommended):

The last major reform of the welfare system occurred during the Clinton administration, and it provided welfare benefits mainly for members of racial minority groups.

  ☐ True   ☐ False

Improved version, with one item on each point (recommended):

The last major reform of the welfare system occurred during the Clinton administration.

  ☐ True   ☐ False

The current welfare system provides benefits mainly for members of racial minority groups.

  ☐ True   ☐ False

Avoid using negative terms such as "not" to create false statements because they can create confusion when combined with the terms "true" and "false." Example 8.7 shows a true–false item made negative with the word "not" and its improved version, which is still false without the word "not."

Example 8.7

A true–false item with the word "not" (not recommended):

Prostate cancer screening is not recommended for older adult males.

  ☐ True   ☐ False

Improved version, without the word "not" (recommended):

Prostate cancer screening is seldom recommended for older adult males.

  ☐ True   ☐ False

Pilot Testing a Test of Knowledge

The pilot test should be conducted with participants who will not be participating in the main study. Calculate the percentage of examinees that marked each item correctly in the pilot test and look for unexpected results. For instance, did some items that seemed simple when they were written turn out to be difficult? If so, it could be that these items have ambiguities or, in the case of multiple-choice items, have poorly written correct choices. Also, did some items that seemed difficult when they were written turn out to be easy? If so, something about the item might have given away the answer such as implausible distracters or other determining factors such as the correct choice being stated more precisely and at greater length than the distracters.

Constructing Questionnaires on Programs and Services

For measuring opinions on programs and services, most researchers conducting surveys prefer objective items.

Planning a Questionnaire on Programs and Services

The proposals for formal programs indicate what services will be provided (for example, group tutoring on job-seeking skills for welfare recipients) and the objectives or outcomes for the clients (for example, getting a job in the private sector). Because programs are funded on the basis of their proposals, it is obvious that programs should be evaluated in terms of the services and objectives specified in their proposals. Thus, when planning a questionnaire, a master list of all services and client objectives should be prepared. If the list is extensive, plan to select those services and client objectives that are deemed most important to be covered in the questionnaire.

Writing Items on Programs and Services

The types of choices provided in an item depends on the content being covered. For some types of content, a simple "yes" or "no" response is all that is needed. Example 8.8 illustrates such content.

Example 8.8

Items requiring only a "yes" or "no" response:

Directions: Think about the <u>last time</u> you visited the clinic. Answer the questions based on that experience.

1. When you called the clinic for an appointment, was the phone answered promptly?   ☐ Yes ☐ No

2. When you arrived for your last appointment, did the receptionist greet you by name?   ☐ Yes ☐ No

3. Were you taken to an examination room within 15 minutes of arriving for your appointment?   ☐ Yes ☐ No

For some types of content, a simple "yes" or "no" response will fail to capture the participants' full reactions. For the content in Example 8.9 on the next page, for instance, it is more appropriate to ask for the degree of satisfaction than simply whether or not the participants were satisfied.

Example 8.9

An item asking for degree of satisfaction (not a yes–no response):

Directions: Think about the <u>last time</u> you visited the clinic. Indicate how satisfied you were with each of the following.

1. The willingness of the doctor to listen to you.
   ☐ Very satisfied
   ☐ Moderately satisfied
   ☐ Somewhat satisfied
   ☐ Somewhat dissatisfied
   ☐ Moderately dissatisfied
   ☐ Very dissatisfied

In the items, be specific in naming characteristics of programs and services. Consider Example 8.10, which shows four items from a questionnaire. Notice that the traits to be evaluated are broad hypothetical constructs, which are inherently ambiguous. What if a professor gets low ratings on flexibility? Should she become more flexible on the requirement that students do homework? Should she become more flexible on the starting time of the class—starting it at different times each week? These types of problems in interpretation can be avoided by asking about specific characteristics, as shown in the Improved Version of Example 8.10.

Example 8.10 (part of a student evaluation questionnaire)

Items with ambiguous terms (not recommended):

Please evaluate your professor in each of the following areas.
(Mark one box across for each item.)

	Excellent	Very good	Fair	Poor	Very poor
1. Flexible	☐	☐	☐	☐	☐
2. Fair	☐	☐	☐	☐	☐
3. Concerned	☐	☐	☐	☐	☐
4. Energetic	☐	☐	☐	☐	☐

Improved Version of Example 8.10 (part of a student evaluation questionnaire)

Items naming specific traits (recommended):

Please evaluate your professor in each of the following areas.

(Mark one box across for each item.)

	Excellent	Very good	Fair	Poor	Very poor
1. Is available to help outside of class.	☐	☐	☐	☐	☐
2. Encourages student participation in class.	☐	☐	☐	☐	☐
3. Uses appropriate tests and measures.	☐	☐	☐	☐	☐
4. Assigns appropriate reading material, including textbooks.	☐	☐	☐	☐	☐

One of the most powerful influences in the marketplace for services and programs is word of mouth—recommending or not recommending a service or program. Thus, an item relating to this matter is often included in questionnaires designed for evaluation of services and programs. Example 8.11 shows an example of such a question.

Example 8.11

An item asking about recommending a service to others (recommended):

Based on your experiences, would you recommend United Parcel Service to others?

☐ Definitely would
☐ Probably would
☐ Maybe would/Maybe not
☐ Probably would not
☐ Definitely would not

Pilot Testing a Questionnaire on Programs and Services

The pilot test should be conducted with participants who will not be participating in the main study. An effective technique is to ask them to "think aloud" as to their reasoning as they answer each question; this can sometimes reveal ambiguities. Also, ask individuals in the pilot test whether they think any of the items are unclear or ambiguous. In addition, ask them if they think any important components of the program or service are missing from the questionnaire.

Constructing Questionnaires on Self-Reported Behaviors

For measuring self-reported behaviors, most researchers conducting surveys prefer objective items.

Planning a Questionnaire on Self-Reported Behaviors

The key to planning a questionnaire on self-reported behaviors is to first draw up a list of the behaviors related to the research purpose. Then, have the list reviewed by others who are knowledgeable of the purpose.

When planning how to measure a behavior, consider whether it can be measured effectively with a single question or would be measured better with a series of items. For instance, suppose a research purpose is to compare smokers and nonsmokers on their knowledge of the effects of smoking on health. A single question asking only "Are you a cigarette smoker?" would probably be insufficient since there are degrees of smoking behavior. Thus, to distinguish regular smokers from incidental smokers, several questions may be required.

Writing Items to Measure Self-Reported Behaviors

Other things being equal, it is best to ask about behaviors over a recent, limited time period. Over a time period such as a week, respondents are more likely to be able to supply accurate answers than over longer periods, such as a month or more. Consider Example 8.12 in which the number of hours "ever used" is asked. The version in Example 8.13 is superior because it is limited to the previous week.

Example 8.12

An item asking if a behavior was ever engaged in (not recommended):

Have you ever used:

E-mail?	☐ No ☐ Yes	If yes, total number of hours ever used: _____
Newsgroups?	☐ No ☐ Yes	If yes, total number of hours ever used: _____
Internet phone?	☐ No ☐ Yes	If yes, total number of hours ever used: _____

Example 8.13

An item asking if a behavior was ever engaged in over a limited, recent time period (recommended):

During the last week, have you used:

E-mail?	☐ No ☐ Yes	If yes, number of hours used last week: _____
Newsgroups?	☐ No ☐ Yes	If yes, number of hours used last week: _____
Internet phone?	☐ No ☐ Yes	If yes, number of hours used last week: _____

Of course, some behaviors are so salient that recall of them will be accurate even if they occurred in the distant past. Examples are: "Were you ever married?" "Have you ever been convicted of a felony?" and "Have you ever served in the United States military?"

When presenting choices for the frequency of behaviors, avoid using vague terms as choices. For instance, in Example 8.14, the choices are vague and, thus, open to interpretation. Example 8.15 is superior because the choices are specific.

Example 8.14

An item with vague choices (not recommended):

How often have you smoked marijuana in the past two weeks?
 ○ Never ○ Sometimes ○ Often ○ Very often

Example 8.15

An item with specific choices (recommended):

How often have you smoked marijuana in the past two weeks?
 ○ Never ○ 1 to 5 times ○ 6 to 10 times ○ 11 to 15 times ○ 16+ times

For some behaviors, it is desirable to provide definitions and examples that help define what is meant by the behavior. For instance, questionnaire item in Box 7B in Chapter 7 defines what is meant by an "alcoholic drink."

Pilot Testing a Questionnaire on Self-Reported Behaviors

The pilot test should be conducted with participants who will not be participating in the main study. Ask them to think aloud about their behaviors as they work through the questions. This may help to identify ambiguities in how the items are stated.

Developing an Interview Schedule

All the instruments discussed so far in this chapter involve written responses (usually by marking choices). Interview schedules (i.e., sets of interview questions) can also be used to measure all the variables mentioned in this chapter.

Semistructured versus Fully Objective Interviews

In a semistructured interview schedule, there is a core set of questions, which can be followed up by probes (i.e., follow-up questions) developed by the interviewer on the spot in response to participants' responses. The process of probing can provide a greater depth of understanding than a fully objective interview.

In fully objective interview schedules, all questions are developed in advance. For each question, participants are presented with choices, and follow-up probes are not used.

For a term-project survey, the fully objective interview is recommended because the resulting data will be easier to analyze than data from a semistructured interview. Nevertheless, students who have experience in analyzing qualitative information may choose to use a semistructured approach.

Planning an Interview Schedule

The process of planning an interview schedule is similar to planning for a paper-and-pencil scale or questionnaire. (See the sections earlier in this chapter on planning measures of various types of traits.)

Writing Interview Questions

When writing objective questions (i.e., questions with choices) for an interview, note that it is more difficult for participants to compare and contrast the choices asked orally than the choices presented in written questions. Thus, it is important to keep the choices for an interview as simple as possible so that they are easy to process mentally. Of course, questions that ask for only "yes" or "no" answers are the easiest to process mentally but they are not always appropriate for all types of content.

One approach to making the mental processing easy for participants is to use the same numerical scale for each question, repeating the scale in each question. Example 8.16 shows three sample questions in which such an approach is used. Note that the first two items express positive sentiments about the object of the attitude, while the third one expresses a negative sentiment. Using both types within a given set of questions is recommended.

Example 8.16

Interview questions with the same numerical scale for each:

1. Interviewer says: On a scale from 1 to 5 with 5 indicating the highest level of agreement, to what extent do you agree with this statement: The research methods course is an important part of my professional training.

2. Interviewer says: On a scale from 1 to 5 with 5 indicating the highest level of agreement, to what extent do you agree with this statement: The research methods course has taught me skills that I will use in my career as a social worker.

3. Interviewer says: On a scale from 1 to 5 with 5 indicating the highest level of agreement, to what extent do you agree with this statement: The skills I am learning in the research methods course have few practical implications.

Pilot Testing an Interview Schedule

The pilot test should be conducted with participants who will not be participating in the main study. During the pilot test, it is important to probe with follow-up questions such as "Can you tell me the reasoning behind your answer?" and "Do you have any other feelings on this issue?" Responses to the probes can provide information that can aid in refining the schedule. Note that using probes in a pilot test is appropriate even if the goal is to refine a schedule that will be fully objective in the main survey.

Avoiding Questions Requiring Ranking

Published instruments seldom ask respondents to rank items according to their relative importance. Likewise, when constructing instruments, students should avoid items requiring ranking.

To understand the problem with ranking, consider Example 8.17, in which classroom teachers are asked to rank three problems.

Example 8.17

An item requiring ranking (not recommended):

Rank the following problems in terms of how important each is in your professional activities as a teacher. Give a rank of "1" to the most important problem, a rank of "2" to the next most important problem, and a rank of "3" to the least important.

_____ Discipline problems in the classroom.
_____ Low parental participation.
_____ Lack of administrative support.

To understand why ranking is not desirable, first consider Teacher A, who has very few problems in the three areas but ranks the problems (as indicated below) based on small perceived differences among them.

Ranks by Teacher A:

___3___ Discipline problems in the classroom.
___2___ Low parental participation.
___1___ Lack of administrative support.

Second, consider Teacher B, who has considerable problems in all three areas, and ranks the problems as follows based on large experienced differences among them.

Ranks by Teacher B:

___3___ Discipline problems in the classroom.
___2___ Low parental participation.
___1___ Lack of administrative support.

Despite the fact that Teachers A and B are quite different, the difference is not revealed by the rankings shown above. This was possible because by asking for rankings, a researcher is only asking for the *relative difference* between the problems. In contrast, more information can be obtained by asking the participants to *rate* instead of rank. For instance, for the rating scale item in Example 8.18, Teacher A might mark "Unimportant" or "Very unimportant" to all three rating scale items, while Teacher B might mark "Important" or "Very important" for all three types of problems. Thus, using a rating scale (instead of asking for rankings) would reveal major differences between the teachers.

Example 8.18

An item requiring rating (improved version of Example 8.17):

Rate the following problems in terms of how important each is in your professional activities as a teacher.

Discipline problems in the classroom.
___Very important   ___Important   ___ Unimportant   ___Very unimportant

Low parental participation.
___Very important   ___Important   ___ Unimportant   ___Very unimportant

Lack of administrative support.
___Very important   ___Important   ___ Unimportant   ___Very unimportant

Concluding Comments

Pilot testing new instruments in order to refine them is an important step and should be mentioned in the research report (see Chapter 14) because it will assure readers that care was taken in developing the new instruments.

Almost all students will want to include items that gather demographic information (i.e., background information) in their instruments. Developing items to gather demographics is covered in the next chapter.

Exercise for Chapter 8

Directions: Will you be developing any of the following? If yes, briefly describe what variables you will be measuring and any difficulties you anticipate in the development of the instrument.

1. Attitude scale

2. Test of knowledge

3. Questionnaire on programs and services

4. Questionnaire on self-reported behaviors

5. Interview schedule

Notes:

Chapter 9

Measuring Demographics

Demographics are background characteristics of the participants such as age, highest level of education, and gender.

There are two reasons for collecting demographics. First, some research problems require it. For instance, if a research purpose is to compare men and women on some variable, gender will need to be determined. The second reason for collecting demographics is to enable a researcher to describe a sample in enough detail that readers of the research report can get a good idea of what types of individuals participated in the survey.

Determining Which Demographics to Collect

There is an almost limitless number of types of demographic information that might be collected. Box 9A on the next page provides a list of some that are commonly examined in surveys.

As a general rule, only demographics deemed to be relevant to the research problem should be collected. For instance, for a survey on voting behavior of students in college elections, the demographics of age, major in college, and political affiliation might be relevant, while health status and hobbies would be peripheral, at best.

For most term-project surveys, consider asking for a maximum of six demographics. More than six demographic items may make the instrument seem unnecessarily long. In addition, a lengthy set of demographic questions might be viewed by participants as an invasion of privacy.

Writing Demographic Questions

Use straightforward language and simple statements and questions to pose demographic questions. The following guidelines address some special issues in posing such questions.

Questions on Sensitive Variables

The impact of requesting information on potentially sensitive matters can be somewhat mitigated by providing a range of values from which participants may choose. For instance, many individuals regard their income as a private matter. Asking participants to indicate the range within which their income falls may make revealing this information more acceptable. Example 9.1 illustrates how this might be done. Notice that the important term "household" is underlined to draw attention to it since individual income is often much lower than household income.

Box 9A   *Sample demographic variables and categories.*[1]

Sample demographic variables for delimiting topics:	Sample categories:
age	elderly
education, classification	gifted
education, highest level of	college graduate
education, type of	vocational
employment, length of	newly hired
employment status	employed part-time
ethnicity/race	Caucasian
extracurricular activities	competitive sports
gender	male
group membership	union member
health, mental disorder	depressed
health, overall status	poor health
health, physical disease	diabetes
hobbies	gardening
household composition	intact family with children
income, household	$20,000 to $35,000
income, personal	high income
language preference	Spanish
marital status	divorced
nationality, current	Canadian
national origin	Mexico
occupation	nurse
place of birth	Korea
political activism	votes regularly
political affiliation	Independent
relationship status	divorced
religion, affiliation	Greek Orthodox
religiosity	attends religious services often
residence, place of	New York City metropolitan area
residence, type of	homeless
sexual orientation	heterosexual
size of city/town/area	large urban area

---

[1] Table reproduced with permission from Pyrczak Publishing from Pan (2004, p. 12).

Example 9.1

A demographic item presenting a range of values (recommended):

What is your approximate <u>household</u> income before taxes?
- ☐ Under $10,000
- ☐ $10,000 to less than $20,000
- ☐ $20,000 to less than $35,000
- ☐ $35,000 to less than $50,000
- ☐ $50,000 to less than $75,000
- ☐ $75,000 to less than $100,000
- ☐ $100,000 or more

When presenting a range of values, be sure to include exhaustive choices (i.e., a set of choices that will include all participants). For instance, in Example 9.2, the choices are not exhaustive because there is no choice for anyone under 18 years of age. The improved item in Example 9.3 starts with the choice "17 years or under."

Example 9.2

A demographic question without exhaustive choices (not recommended):

What is your age?
- ☐ 18–24 years
- ☐ 25–44 years
- ☐ 45–64 years
- ☐ 65 years or over

Example 9.3

An improved version of Example 9.2:

What is your age?
- ☐ 17 years or under
- ☐ 18–24 years
- ☐ 25–44 years
- ☐ 45–64 years
- ☐ 65 years or over

When presenting a range of values, consider how many individuals are likely to fall into each range. For instance, for a survey of undergraduates, the item in Example 9.3 above would likely have the vast majority of respondents in the second range of values (18 to 24), with only a scattering above and below this range. For such a population, more differentiation among the participants in terms of age could be obtained with the choices in Example 9.4.[2]

---

[2] Note that for undergraduates, age is less sensitive an issue than for older adults, so age might be asked with an open-ended question.

Example 9.4

An improved version of Example 9.2 for undergraduates:

What is your age?

☐ 17 years or under

☐ 18–19 years

☐ 20–21 years

☐ 22–23 years

☐ 24 years or over

A potentially sensitive issue is racial and ethnic background. The difficulty in writing items on this variable arises because preferred terms change over time and because various members of the same group may prefer different terms. In Example 9.5, which was used in a questionnaire prepared by an insurance company, alternative terms are provided within three of the choices (e.g., Black/African American) to accommodate changing preferences for terms. Notice that the choice for "Other" would allow participants to indicate mixed ancestry.

Example 9.5

Demographic items on race/ethnicity with alternative terms for race/ethnicity in three choices:

Which of the following best describes your racial or ethnic background?
Please check one.

☐ Asian

☐ Black/African American

☐ White/Caucasian

☐ Hispanic (may be any race)

☐ Native American/American Indian

☐ Other. Please specify: _____

Because it is difficult to write satisfactory items on race/ethnicity, it is helpful to examine how professional survey researchers have written such items. Example 9.6 shows an item used by the United States Census Bureau in the last census. Notice that even with such a detailed item, the bureau has allowed for individuals to print the name of some "other" group.

Example 9.6

Demographic item used by the Census Bureau:

Is Person 1 Spanish/Hispanic/Latino?

Mark ☒ in the **"No"** box if **not** Spanish/Hispanic/Latino.

☐ **No,** not Spanish/Hispanic/Latino   ☐ Yes, Puerto Rican

☐ Yes, Mexican, Mexican Am., Chicano   ☐ Yes, Cuban

☐ Yes, other Spanish/Hispanic/Latino – *Print group*:

Providing Definitions

Carefully consider all terms in demographic questions to determine if definitions or explanations should be provided. It is especially important to provide these when using technical terms with which participants may not be fully familiar. For instance, in a study of breast cancer survivors, researchers requested demographics on a number of variables such as current age, prior health status, and age at diagnosis. In addition, they asked about the type of cancer using three technical terms (i.e., localized, regional, and invasive). They provided explanations of the terms, as indicated in Example 9.7.

Example 9.7

Explanations offered for technical terms:[3]

Type of cancer was assessed by asking women whether they had localized, regional, or invasive disease, with the following explanations: local = no lymph nodes are involved; regional = cancer has spread past the breast to the underarm lymph nodes; and invasive = cancer has spread beyond the underarm lymph nodes.

Providing Exhaustive Choices

As mentioned earlier, the choices in an item should be exhaustive (i.e., provide a choice for each possibility). Sometimes, it is difficult to spot deficiencies in the exhaustiveness of the choices. Consider Example 9.8, which at first glance may seem adequate. Notice, however, that there is no choice for a participant who did not finish elementary school. In addition, the choice "college graduate" is ambiguous because it is not clear if it includes graduates of two-year colleges. In contrast, consider Example 9.9, which shows how the United States Census Bureau asked about highest level of education completed. Example 9.9 is clearly superior to Example 9.8 because Example 9.9 has exhaustive choices, and each choice is defined by indicating the number of years associated with it.

---

[3] Bellizzi, K. M., & Blank, T. O. (2006). Predicting posttraumatic growth in breast cancer survivors. *Health Psychology, 25,* 47–56.

Example 9.8

Demographic item that fails to provide exhaustive choices and is ambiguous:

Highest level of education completed:

☐ Elementary

☐ Secondary

☐ Some college

☐ College graduate

Example 9.9

Improved version (Census Bureau version) of Example 9.8:

Highest level of education completed:

☐ Elementary (0 to 8 years)

☐ Some high school (1 to 3 years)

☐ High school graduate (4 years)

☐ Some college (1 to 3 years)

☐ College graduate (4 or more years)

Providing Spaces for Responses to Open-Ended Questions

As a general rule, choices that participants can quickly check off should be provided. However, for some items of information, there may be so many possible choices that providing choices would be unwieldy. For instance, asking participants for zip codes is best done with an open-ended question because there are so many possible zip codes. Consider Example 9.10. Note that five boxes are provided, one for each number in a basic zip code (i.e., the zip code without a four-number extension).

Example 9.10

An open-ended question with boxes for the answer:

What is the zip code for your residence? Write one number in each box.

For non-numerical entries, such as words that may vary greatly in the number of letters (or even the number of words) in response to an open-ended item, be careful to provide an appropriate amount of space. Too much or two little space might confuse participants. For instance, for the question, "What is the name of your neighborhood?" posed to residents of Los Angeles, more than one or two lines of space might suggest that the researcher is seeking more than a simple answer such as "Wilshire District."

Pilot Testing Demographic Questions

A pilot test of the demographic questions should be conducted with individuals who will not be participating in the main survey. An effective way to pilot test is to ask each individual to "think aloud" as they consider and respond to the questions. Often, this can reveal flaws in demographic questions. For instance, in response to the question, "Are you in a relationship?" a pilot study participant might state this thought, "I've been dating someone for two weeks. I wonder if that counts as a relationship." Such a statement would suggest that the term "relationship" needs to be defined within the item.

Organizing and Introducing Demographic Questions

Whether presented in a questionnaire or in an interview schedule, all demographic items should be grouped together and placed at the end of the questionnaire or schedule. This is recommended because when demographic questions are asked first, they blur the purpose of the instrument (making the questionnaire or schedule seem insignificant) and may be viewed as intrusive, especially if sensitive demographics are sought.

Just before asking the demographic questions, a brief explanation should be given for asking them. For instance, in an interview, the interviewer might state, "Now, I have a few questions about your background. This information is needed for the statistical analysis and categorization of your answers." Giving participants an explanation helps blunt resistance to answering questions that some participants might view as invasive of their privacy.[4]

Exercise for Chapter 9

Directions: Share your answers to this exercise with other students who may still be considering which demographic questions to ask and how to phrase them.

1. List demographic variables that might help readers of your research report visualize relevant characteristics of your sample.

2. Are any of the variables you listed in response to Question 1 potentially sensitive? Might participants view questions about them as an invasion of privacy? Explain.

---

[4] Note that assurances of confidentiality and anonymity should be given at the beginning of the questionnaire or interview, which are discussed in the next chapter. If some demographic questions are especially sensitive, these assurances might be repeated just before the demographic questions are asked.

3. Write two demographic questions you intend to ask in your survey. Have them reviewed by other students and rewrite the questions based on suggestions the students make for improving them.

Chapter 10

Administering Instruments

This chapter provides guidelines on the administration of instruments. It covers both questionnaires and interviews.

Preparing Instruments for Administration

Before administering an instrument, the following steps should be taken in order to make it an efficient and effective measurement tool.

Give a Questionnaire a Title

A questionnaire should be given a title that clearly indicates the types of variables covered. An informative title helps participants develop an appropriate mind-set for answering the questions. Consider a questionnaire for a survey in which the researcher wants to compare the political activism (e.g., voting, signing petitions, attending demonstrations) of undergraduates majoring in political science with that of undergraduates with other majors. The title in Example 10.1 is inadequate because it could apply to any number of issues. The title in Example 10.2 is superior.

Example 10.1

A vague questionnaire title (not recommended):

Undergraduate Opinion Survey

Example 10.2

A questionnaire title that names a specific variable (recommended):

Undergraduates' Political Activism Survey

Prepare an Introduction

Whether a questionnaire or an interview is being used, participants should be given a brief introduction, which should indicate (a) the purpose of the survey, (b) the sponsor (e.g., in the case of a term-project survey, the sponsor is the student conducting the survey), (c) the approximate amount of time it will take to complete the questionnaire or interview, and (d) whether responses will remain confidential. This is illustrated in Example 10.3.

Example 10.3

A brief introduction for a questionnaire or interview:

The purpose of this survey is to explore undergraduates' current and future levels of participation in political processes. I am conducting this survey as part of a term project for my course in political science methodology. The survey will take less than five minutes of your time, and your cooperation will be greatly appreciated. Your responses will remain confidential, and the research report will present only group averages and percentages.

When stating the purpose of the survey, point out any potential benefits that might accrue either to the individual responding or to some group of individuals. For instance, in the introduction to a questionnaire on college reference-room services, a researcher might point out that the information collected through the survey might help in restructuring the services to the benefit of all students who use the library.

Group the Items by Topic

If there is more than one question on each of several topics, group the items by topic. In a questionnaire, provide subheadings for each group of questions, such as those in Example 10.4. In an interview schedule, introduce each group with a statement such as, "First, I have a few questions about your selection of a health plan."

Example 10.4

Subheadings for groups of questions:

About Your Selection of a Health Plan (3 questions)

About Your Primary Care Physician (5 questions)

About Specialists (3 questions)

About Prescription Drugs (4 questions)

Demographics (6 questions)

Conclude with a "Thank You" and Contact Information

The instrument should end with a thank-you statement. In addition, because participants should be treated as "participants" and not "objects" or "subjects," they should be informed of how to contact the researcher in the future if they have any concerns or desire feedback on the results.

Group Administration of Questionnaires

Sometimes questionnaires are administered to groups of individuals such as all members of a class. Because potential participants should be given the right to decline to participate, determine in advance what individuals who decline should be instructed to do while waiting for other students who are participating. Should they be asked to wait quietly at their desks during the administration? Should they be told they are free to leave the classroom for a specified number of minutes?

Advantage of Group Administration

Administering a questionnaire to one or more groups (such as class sections) is an efficient way to obtain a large sample.

Disadvantage of Group Administration

Naturally existing groups, such as class sections of a sociology course, are called "clusters." (See the information on cluster sampling in Chapter 6.) Each cluster tends to be homogeneous in important respects. For instance, an evening section of the course might have older students who are employed full time during the day. Thus, the responses from such a group might not represent the full diversity of students taking sociology courses.

Individual Administration of Questionnaires

Questionnaires can be handed out to individuals instead of groups. For instance, a researcher could set up a small table outside buildings on campus and solicit individual respondents to have a seat at the table and respond to the questionnaire.

Advantage of Individual Administration

Administering a questionnaire to individuals usually will provide a more diverse sample than administration to naturally existing groups. (See the "Disadvantage of Group Administration" above.)

Disadvantage of Individual Administration

Administration to one individual at a time will take more effort and time than administration to groups.

Administration of Questionnaires by Mail

Mailing questionnaires for a survey has important advantages and serious disadvantages. Because of the disadvantages discussed below, mailing questionnaires for a term-project survey is not generally recommended. Nevertheless, some students may have the resources to use the mailed survey technique, especially if they can obtain permission to use the campus mail free or at a low charge.

Advantage of Administering Questionnaires by Mail

The major advantage of the mailed survey is that it allows researchers to easily reach beyond their own limited geographical area. This can result in diversity in sampling that otherwise might be impossible to obtain.

Disadvantages of Administering Questionnaires by Mail

An obvious disadvantage is the cost of mailing questionnaires and paying for the return postage. In addition, there are three other disadvantages.

First, mailed surveys have notoriously low response rates. Box 10A shows the response rates researchers reported for some recently published surveys. Note that these are published surveys. Because surveys with low response rates are less likely to be published than surveys with high response rates, this sample of response rates may be biased toward studies with higher than average response rates.[1] Some techniques researchers use in an effort to increase response rates to mailed surveys are listed in Box 10B.

The second disadvantage of mailed surveys is that responses can trickle in over a period of weeks, which might push a term-project survey over the time limits for the semester.

The third disadvantage is that several mailings are usually required (e.g., remailing questionnaires to nonrespondents to the first mailing) in order to obtain a reasonably high response rate. Box 10A indicates the number of mailings for each survey cited. As you can see, there is a rough pattern in which studies with more mailings tend to have higher response rates. Unfortunately, for a term project, second and third mailings can extend the time line beyond a single semester, and increase the costs, which may be out of students' ranges.

Box 10A *A sample of response rates to mailed surveys.*

> 1. Number of mailings: **one.** Response rate: **26%.**
>   Reference: Phillips, K. M., & Brandon, T. H. (2004). Do psychologists adhere to the clinical practice guidelines for tobacco cessation? A survey of practitioners. *Professional Psychology: Research and Practice, 35,* 281–285.
>
> 2. Number of mailings: **one.** Response rate: **28%.**
>   Reference: Kazantzis, N., Lampropoulos, G. K., & Deane, F. P. (2005). A national survey of practicing psychologists' use and attitudes toward homework in psychotherapy. *Journal of Consulting and Clinical Psychology, 73,* 742–748.
>
> 3. Number of mailings: **one.** Response rate: **39%.**
>   Reference: Stenzel. C. L., & Rupert, P. A. (2004). Psychologists' use of touch in individual psychotherapy. *Psychotherapy: Theory, Research, Practice, Training, 41,* 332–345.
>
> *(Continued on next page)*

---

[1] The sample of published surveys in Box 10A was obtained by searching the *PsycARTICLES* database using these search criteria: the term "survey" in the title *or* the term "survey" in the abstract. Of the articles identified, only those that clearly stated a single response rate (not rates for various subgroups) were selected.

Box 10A   *(Continued)*

4. Number of mailings: **one**. Response rate: **40%**.

   Reference: Rosenberg, J. I., Getzelman, M. A., Arcinue, F., & Oren, C. Z. (2005). An exploratory look at students' experiences of problematic peers in academic professional psychology programs. *Professional Psychology: Research and Practice, 36*, 665–673.

5. Number of mailings: **two**. Response rate: **39%**.

   Reference: Humbke, K. L., Brown, D. L., Welder, A. N., Fillion, D. T., Dobson, K. S., & Arnett, J. L. (2004). A survey of hospital psychology in Canada. *Canadian Psychology, 45*, 31–41.

6. Number of mailings: **two**. Response rate: **44%**.

   Reference: Williams, R. M., Turner, A. P., Hatzakis, M., Chu, S., Rodriguez, A. A., Bowen, J. D., & Haselkorn, J. K. (2004). Social support among veterans with Multiple Sclerosis. *Rehabilitation Psychology, 49*, 106–113.

7. Number of mailings: **three**. Response rate: **45%**.

   Reference: Helbok, C. M., Marinelli, R. P., & Walls, R. T. (2006). National survey of ethical practices across rural and urban communities. *Professional Psychology: Research and Practice, 37*, 36–44.

8. Number of mailings: **three**. Response rate: **46%**.

   Reference: Adams, R. E., Boscarino, J. A., & Figley, C. R. (2006). Compassion fatigue and psychological distress among social workers: A validation study. *American Journal of Orthopsychiatry, 76*, 103–108.

9. Number of mailings: **three**. Response rate: **49%**.

   Reference: Levine, E. S., & Schmelkin, L. P. (2006). The move to prescribe: A change in paradigm? *Professional Psychology: Research and Practice, 37*, 205–209.

Box 10B   *Techniques for increasing response rates to mailed surveys.*

1. Include a self-addressed stamped envelope for replies.

2. Offer an incentive, such as a chance to win a prize in a drawing.

3. Mail an advance postcard, indicating that a survey will be arriving in the mail soon. This helps to establish that the mailed survey is not junk mail.

4. Use professional-looking stationery, such as university stationery (with permission).

5. Put a blurb on the outside of the envelope to encourage individuals to open it.

6. Keep the questionnaire as short and straightforward as possible.

7. Send follow-up mailings to nonrespondents.

Administration of Questionnaires by E-mail

Students who have access to relevant lists of e-mail addresses might consider administration by e-mail. For instance, various organizations on campuses maintain e-mail addresses of their members. These lists might be made available for use in a survey on a topic of interest to the members.

For administration via e-mail, the recommended procedure is to send an e-mail letter soliciting participation with a link at the end of the letter on which respondents can click to get to the Internet site that contains the questionnaire. Pay special attention to the subject line for the e-mail letter. A subject line such as "Your opinions are needed" is vague and may make the e-mail appear to be junk mail. An e-mail with a more specific subject line such as "Foreign Student Services Survey at JFK University" might be more likely to be opened by respondents who belong to an association of foreign students than the one with a vague subject line.

Advantages of Administering a Questionnaire by E-mail

An obvious advantage is that it is inexpensive to contact a large number of potential respondents via e-mail. In addition, a geographically diverse sample can be contacted. Also, community-based samples (as opposed to campus samples) can be efficiently contacted.

Disadvantages of Administering Questionnaires by E-mail

Administration via e-mail requires technical skills that may be more advanced than those possessed by many students conducting a term project. In addition, e-mail surveys can have high rates of nonresponse, which is also a disadvantage of mailed surveys.

Administration of Interviews by Telephone

Under limited circumstances, a list of telephone numbers for a population might be available to student researchers. For instance, a community political organization may make telephone numbers of their members available for surveys that have the potential to advance their cause.

Another possibility is to use random digit dialing (RDD). In this technique, digits are selected at random within selected area codes, which roughly correspond to geographical areas. RDD overcomes the problem posed by the fact that many individuals have unlisted telephone numbers. Note that those who have listed numbers may be systematically different in a number of important ways from those with unlisted numbers. (See the section on simple random sampling in Chapter 6 to review how to obtain lists of random digits.)

Advantages of Administering Interviews by Telephone

Administration of interviews by telephone allows researchers to obtain a quick snapshot of opinions and attitudes across a diverse geographical area. For instance, immediately after a debate by candidates for governor of a state, teams of interviewers can call hundreds of voters to ask for their opinions on the candidates' performances, which can be reported in the news media very soon afterward. Students conducting term-project surveys seldom have need for such speed.

Disadvantages of Administering Interviews by Telephone

Administration of interviews by telephone can be expensive, which may rule out its use by students conducting term projects. Also, by their very nature, interviews (whether by telephone or not) are labor intensive, typically requiring more time than administration of questionnaires. Administration by telephone for a term-project survey is not recommended.

Administration of Face-to-Face Interviews

Face-to-face interviews may be conducted for term-project surveys. Plan in advance how potential participants will be selected. For instance, every tenth individual leaving certain classroom buildings on campus might be approached. Also, plan exactly what will be said when soliciting respondents because using varying appeals with different potential participants may differentially affect how they respond.

Advantages of Face-to-Face Interviews

Participation rates when potential participants are approached on a face-to-face basis can be higher than when they receive an impersonal mailed questionnaire. In addition, an interviewer might get insights into participants' understanding of the interview questions through comments and facial expressions. For instance, some respondents may express difficulty in understanding what a question is driving at, which might be noted in the research report with a suggestion that the question be reworded in future studies.

Disadvantages of Face-to-Face Interviews

By their very nature, face-to-face interviews are typically more labor intensive than the administration of questionnaires. For classes in which groups of students are permitted to work jointly on term-project surveys, the labor might be shared by members of the group.

Exercise for Chapter 10

1. If you will be using a questionnaire, write a title for it and ask other students to provide feedback on it.

2. Prepare a brief introduction for your questionnaire or interview schedule.

3. If you will be using a questionnaire, which of the following methods do you plan for administration? Explain the reason for your choice.

   A. Group administration

   B. Individual administration

   C. Mail

   D. E-mail

4. If you will be using an interview schedule, which of the following methods do you plan for administration? Explain the reason for your choice.

   A. Telephone

   B. Face-to-face

Chapter 11

Analysis: Percentages

A percentage is calculated by dividing the part by the whole and multiplying by 100. For instance, if 30 out of 75 respondents rate a product as being excellent, then 40% rate it as excellent (i.e., $30/75 = .40 \times 100\% = 40\%$). This chapter describes how to present percentages as well as the calculation and presentation of margins of error for percentages.

When to Use Percentages

Percentages are usually the statistic of choice for presenting *categorical data* (also known as *nominal data*). Categorical data consist of sets of categories with names (not numbers) that have no numerical sequence. For instance, political affiliation is a categorical variable with categories such as Democrat, Republican, Independent, and Other. These categories are not measured on a numerical scale.

Some variables are not categorical, such as scores on an attitude scale from 0 to 50, where 0 is the lowest attitude and 50 is the highest. Typically, such data are summarized using means and standard deviations, which are discussed in the next chapter.

Presenting Percentages

This section describes how to present percentages in the results section of a research report.

Presentation in Sentences versus Tables

When there are a limited number of percentages, they can be presented in sentences in the results section of a research report. This is illustrated in Example 11.1. Note that when reporting percentages, the number of cases (i.e., frequencies) underlying the percentages is often reported. The symbol *n* stands for "number of cases."

Example 11.1
Presenting percentages in sentences:

The sources of fear reported by the fifth-grade children, in order, are "violence" (70%, $n = 140$), "death" (50%, $n = 100$), "animals" (40%, $n = 80$), "school" (20%, $n = 40$), and "other" (10%, $n = 20$). Because each child was permitted to name more than one source of fear, the percentages sum to more than 100.

Even with as few as five percentages for a variable (e.g., sources of fear), presentation in a table, such as Table 11.A in Example 11.2, can be more effective than presenting the percentages in sentences. Note that when tables are used, they should be referred to in the text before the table is presented. For instance, in Example 11.2, the text provides a rough summary of the percentages in the table and specifically refers readers to the table (i.e., "see Table 11.A").

Example 11.2

Percentages presented in a table with a comment introducing the table:

The text says: A majority of the fifth-graders reported fear of violence and death, while less than 50% reported fear of animals and school (see Table 11.A).

Table 11.A

Sources of Fear Reported by Fifth-Grade Children (n = 200)

Violence	Death	Animals	School	Other
70%	60%	40%	20%	10%
($n = 140$)	($n = 120$)	($n = 80$)	($n = 40$)	($n = 20$)

Note. Each child was permitted to name more than one source of fear. Thus, percentages sum to more than 100%.

Presentation in Two-Way Contingency Tables

A *contingency table* is a two-way table that summarizes the participants' responses to two categorical variables. For instance, consider Table 11.B in Example 11.3, which shows a perfect relationship between current smoking status and opinions on restricting smoking. All those who do not currently smoke favor restrictions, while all those who do currently smoke oppose restrictions, making the relationship perfect.

Example 11.3

A contingency with a perfect relationship between two variables:

Table 11.B

Contingency Table with Frequencies for a Group of Respondents

		Favors restrictions on smoking in public	
		Yes	No
Smoking currently?	Yes	0	100%
	No	100%	0

Of course, results are almost never as clear-cut as in Example 11.3. Example 11.4 shows a more realistic example, in which there is a relationship that is less perfect. However, it still indicates a relationship. Specifically, those who use the Internet more frequently are more opposed to censorship of material on the Internet than those who use it less frequently.[1]

Example 11.4

Contingency table with a less than perfect relationship between two variables:

Table 11.C

Contingency table with frequencies for a group of respondents

		Frequency of Internet use		
		Frequent	Occasional	Seldom
Favors censorship of material on the Internet?	Yes	20% ($n = 60$)	30% ($n = 90$)	50% ($n = 150$)
	No	50% ($n = 150$)	30% ($n = 90$)	20% ($n = 60$)

Using Percentages to Compare Groups

Up to this point in this chapter, the use of percentages to describe a single group of participants has been illustrated in Examples 11.1 through 11.4. Percentages can also be used to compare two or more groups. For instance, the percentages in Table 11.D in Example 11.5 facilitate a comparison of the ages of men and women in a sample.

Example 11.5

Use of percentages to describe scores:

Table 11.D

Ages of Respondents By Gender

Age	Men ($n = 830$)	Women ($n = 723$)
18 years and under	4.8% ($n = 40$)	8.7% ($n = 63$)
19–24 years	9.9% ($n = 82$)	13.3% ($n = 96$)
25–34 years	18.2% ($n = 151$)	25.4% ($n = 184$)
35–44 years	22.8% ($n = 189$)	19.4% ($n = 140$)
45–54 years	20.0% ($n = 166$)	15.4% ($n = 111$)
55–64 years	13.7% ($n = 114$)	13.8% ($n = 100$)
65–74 years	5.3% ($n = 44$)	2.6% ($n = 19$)
75 years and over	5.3% ($n = 44$)	1.4% ($n = 10$)
Total	100.0%	100.0%

---

[1] Students who have taken statistics will recognize that the data in Example 11.4 could be analyzed with a chi-square test to determine the statistical significance of the relationship. See Appendix C for guidelines on significance testing. Also, the degree of relationship could be expressed with Cramer's *V*, which is beyond the scope of this book but is covered in most introductory statistics textbooks.

Margins of Error for Percentages

Margins of error indicate the number of points to allow for when interpreting results in light of random sampling errors. These sampling errors occur because, by the luck of the draw, a sample drawn from a population may not be representative. Fortunately, margins of error for percentages are easy to calculate, as indicated below.[2]

The 68% Margin of Error

The formula for the 68% margin of error is shown in Example 11.6[3]

Example 11.6

Calculation of the 68% margin of error for a percentage:

In response to a questionnaire item, 75% of a simple random sample of 100 teachers in a school district reported that they feel very competent using the Internet to obtain information. To calculate the margin of error, the following formula was used, where *P* is the percentage who reported feeling competent (i.e., 75), *Q* is 100 minus *P* (i.e., 100 − 75 = 25), and *n* is the number of respondents (i.e., 100).

$$S_P = \sqrt{\frac{PQ}{n}} = \sqrt{\frac{(75)(25)}{100}} = \sqrt{\frac{1,875}{100}} = \sqrt{18.75} = 4.33$$

For reasons that are beyond the scope of this book, the standard error of a percentage when calculated as shown in Example 11.6 is a *68% margin of error*. That is, although 75% of the sample said they felt very competent using the Internet, the researcher can be only 68% confident that the *true percentage in the whole population* that feels very competent lies within 4.33 percentage points of 75%.

The 95% Margin of Error and Confidence Interval

The 68% margin of error can be manipulated to obtain a margin with any desired degree of confidence.

The most commonly used margin is the *95% margin of error*. This is easy to obtain: Simply multiply the 68% margin of error by 1.96. Thus, for Example 11.6 above, the 95% margin of error equals 4.33 × 1.96 = 8.48. (Note that the 1.96 is a constant; use it for all problems of this type regardless of the values of your specific results.)

The 95% margin of error can be used to build a *95% confidence interval* (95% C.I.). A confidence interval consists of two values. The first value is obtained by *subtracting* the

---

[2] Note that margins of error apply only to errors created by random sampling. These margins do not apply to errors created by bias in sampling, since each bias has its own unknown characteristics.
[3] In this chapter, we will be considering margins of error for *simple random sampling*. The margins may be slightly different if other sampling methods are used such as *stratified random sampling*. The method presented here is precise only for samples of 60 or more respondents, but provide a rough approximation for samples as small as 15.

margin of error from the percentage in question (75% – 8.48% = 66%). The second value is obtained by *adding* the margin of error to the percentage in question (75% + 8.48% = 83%). Example 11.7 shows how the confidence interval might be reported in the results section of a research report.

Example 11.7

Reporting a percentage with its 95% confidence interval:

In response to a questionnaire item, 75% of a simple random sample of 100 teachers in a school district reported that they feel very competent using the Internet to obtain information (95% C.I. = 66%–83%).

The Margins of Error and Sample Size

Based on the sample of 100 in Example 11.7, the best estimate is that the percentage who feel competent is 75%, but a researcher needs to allow more than 8 percentage points (specifically, 8.48 points for 95% confidence) on each side of this estimate for the possible effects of random errors produced by random sampling. With a margin of 8 percentage points, the result is not very precise. How can a researcher get more precise results? By using a larger sample. This is illustrated in Example 11.8 where another researcher used a sample of 1,000. As you can see, with a sample of 1,000, the 68% margin of error is only 1.37 points (instead of 4.33 when a sample of 100 was used), and the more commonly used 95% margin of error is only 2.69 points (instead of 8.48 when a sample of 100 was used).

Example 11.8

Illustration of the effects of sample size on the margin of error:

A researcher conducted the same study as the one in Example 11.6 and obtained the same result: 75% of the sample indicated that they feel very competent using the Internet to obtain information. However, this researcher used a sample of 1,000 respondents and thus obtained much smaller margins of error than the first researcher. Here are the calculations for the second researcher:

$$S_P = \sqrt{\frac{PQ}{n}} = \sqrt{\frac{(75)(25)}{1,000}} = \sqrt{\frac{1,875}{1,000}} = \sqrt{1.87} = 1.37$$

Thus, the 68% margin of error is only 1.37 points (instead of 4.33 for the researcher who sampled only 100 teachers). For the 95% margin of error, multiply this result (1.37) by 1.96, which yields only 2.69 as the 95% margin of error (instead of 8.48 for the researcher who sampled only 100 teachers).

Exercise for Chapter 11

1. In your research report, do you plan to present percentages for any of the variables in your survey? If yes, name the variables.

2. In your research report, do you plan to present any two-way contingency tables with percentages? If yes, what variables will be in each contingency table?

3. In your research report, do you plan to present margins of error for percentages? If yes, will you be reporting 95% confidence intervals?

Chapter 12

Analysis: Averages and Measures of Variability

This chapter describes when to use the two most commonly reported averages (the *mean* and *median*) as well as the two most common measures of variability (the *standard deviation* and the *interquartile range*). When the mean is reported as the average, it is customary to also report the standard deviation. When the median is reported as the average, the *interquartile range* is also customarily reported. This chapter defines each of these statistics, describes when to use them, how to compute them, and how to present them in a research report.

When to Use the Mean

The mean is used for describing the average of a set of scores. There are three conditions under which the mean should *not* be used: (a) when the data are nominal, in which case percentages should be used, as discussed in the previous chapter; (b) when the data are highly skewed, which is illustrated later in this chapter; and (c) when the data consist of ranks. Note that Chapter 8 suggests avoiding instruments that produce ranked data, so the analysis of ranks will not be discussed further in this book.

Computing the Mean

The mean is computed by summing the scores and dividing by the number of scores. For instance, if five respondents to a survey reported their ages as 20, 21, 25, 29, and 31, the mean age is $20 + 21 + 25 + 29 + 31 = 126/5 = 25.2$.

Presenting Means in a Research Report

When there are several means, it is usually best to present them in a table such as the one in Example 12.1. Note that the symbol for the mean of a sample is *m*, while the symbol for the mean for an entire population is *M*. In the following example, *M* is used because all faculty members serving under the department chair participated in the survey.

Example 12.1

A table with means:

Table 12.A

Mean Ratings on Effectiveness of a Department Chair on a Scale from 0 (Very Ineffective) to 3 (Very Effective)

Item	M
1. Demonstrates leadership in curricular development and revision	1.86
2. Demonstrates leadership in the recruitment, selection, and retention of highly qualified faculty	2.76
3. Schedules classes to maximize faculty and other resources	2.05
4. Is available to faculty and staff	1.40
5. Provides for effective function of the division office	2.33
6. Involves faculty, where appropriate, in department decision making	1.99

When to Use the Standard Deviation

When the mean is reported as the average, it is conventional to also report the standard deviation. While the mean is an average, the standard deviation is a *measure of variability*.

The term *variability* refers to the extent to which respondents vary or differ from each other. Examining the scores and statistics for the three groups in Example 12.2 illustrates the meaning of variability. First, notice that all three groups have the same mean but different standard deviations. Note that the symbol for the standard deviation is *S* or *SD*.[1]

Example 12.2

Means and standard deviations for three groups of scores:

Attitude scores for Group A: 15, 15, 15, 15, 15, 15, 15
$M = 15.00, S = 0.00$

Attitude scores for Group B: 14, 14, 14, 15, 16, 16, 16
$M = 15.00, S = 0.93$

Attitude scores for Group C: 0, 5, 10, 15, 20, 25, 30
$M = 15.00, S = 10.00$

As you can see in Example 12.2, Group A has no variability among its scores (i.e., all the scores are the same), which is indicated by its standard deviation of 0.00. Group B has a little more variability among its scores than Group A, as indicated by its standard deviation of 0.93. Group C has much more variability than either Group A or Group B. (Notice there are large differences among Group C's scores.) The much larger variability among Group C's

---

[1] The uppercase *S* or *SD* indicates that the standard deviation is based on a study of a population, while the lowercase *s* or *sd* indicates that the standard deviation is based on a sample.

scores is indicated by its standard deviation of 10.00. Thus, the example shows that the larger the differences among the scores, the larger the standard deviation will be.

What makes a standard deviation large or small? The precise answer is how far the scores are from the mean of the group. When all the scores are the same as the mean, such as Group A's scores in Example 12.2, the standard deviation is zero. When the scores differ greatly from their mean, which is the case for Group C (for example, scores such as 0, 5, 25, and 30 are far from the mean of 15.00), the standard deviation will be large.

Computing the Standard Deviation

Table 12.B in Example 12.3 is a worktable for the computation of the standard deviation. To use the worktable, first list the scores in the first column of a table. Second, subtract the mean (15.00) from each score, yielding the *difference scores*. Third, square each difference score as shown in the last column of the table. Fourth, sum the scores as shown in the last column. After constructing a table such as the one in Example 12.3, enter the values as shown in the formula below the table.

Example 12.3

Computation of the standard deviation:

Table 12.B

Worktable for Computing the Standard Deviation

A score	minus	the mean	equals	the difference.	Then, square the difference.
0	–	15	=	–15	225
5	–	15	=	–10	100
10	–	15	=	–5	25
15	–	15	=	0	0
20	–	15	=	5	25
25	–	15	=	10	100
30	–	15	=	15	225
					Total = 700

To get the standard deviation, use this formula, in which the *total* is the sum of the last column in Table 12.B (in this case, 700), and N is the number of cases (in this case, 7 since there are 7 scores):

$$S = \sqrt{\frac{total}{N}} = \sqrt{\frac{700}{7}} = \sqrt{100} = 10.0$$

The formula on the previous page should be used when an entire population has been studied. To compute the standard deviation when only a sample has been studied, use the following slightly modified formula:[2]

$$s = \sqrt{\frac{total}{n-1}} = \sqrt{\frac{700}{7-1}} = \sqrt{116.67} = 10.80$$

The Standard Deviation and the Normal Curve

The normal curve is a bell-shaped distribution that is found very widely in nature. For instance, the heights of women (or men) in large populations are distributed normally, the weights of diamonds found in nature are distributed normally, and the length of monkeys' arms are distributed normally. Likewise, mental traits such as achievement and attitudes are often normally distributed.

The standard deviation has this special relationship to the normal curve: *68% of the respondents lies within one standard deviation unit of the mean* (i.e., the mean plus/minus the standard deviation). For instance, if a researcher stated in a research report that *M* = 70 and *S* = 10 for a normal distribution of responses, the reader would know that 68% of the respondents have scores between 60 (i.e., the mean of 70 minus the standard deviation of 10) and 80 (i.e., the mean of 70 plus the standard deviation of 10). This is illustrated in Figure 12.A in Example 12.4.

Example 12.4

Figure illustrating that 68% of the cases lies within one standard deviation unit of the mean in a normal distribution:

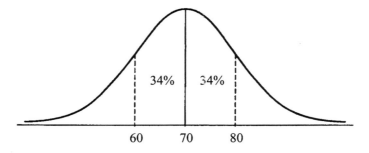

Figure 12.A. Normal curve with mean of 70 and a standard deviation of 10.00.

---

[2] The only difference is subtracting the constant 1 in the denominator. You may recall that researchers use uppercase letters for statistics based on populations and lowercase letters for statistics based on samples. Thus, the first formula for the standard deviation presented above has an uppercase *N* in it, while the second formula has a lowercase *n*.

Presenting Standard Deviations in a Research Report

In a research report, the corresponding standard deviation is usually presented immediately after each mean is presented. Example 12.5 shows how this can be done in a sentence.

Example 12.5

Means and standard deviations presented in a sentence:

Political activism was measured on a scale from 1 to 20. On average, seniors reported much more political activism ($m = 13.5$, $s = 2.4$) than juniors ($m = 8.3$, $s = 1.5$), sophomores ($m = 7.0$, $s = 1.7$), or freshmen ($m = 8.5$, $s = 1.8$). In addition, the seniors were more variable than the other groups in their activism, as indicated by the standard deviations.

When there are several means and standard deviations, it is usually more effective to present them in a table with some textual material summarizing the statistics in the table. This is illustrated in Example 12.6.

Example 12.6

Means and standard deviations presented in a table:

The text says: Political activism was measured on a scale from 1 to 20. On average, seniors reported much more political activism than the other three groups. In addition, the seniors were more variable than the other groups in their activism, as indicated by the standard deviations. See Table 12.C.

Table 12.C

Means and Standard Deviations for Four Groups

Seniors	Juniors	Sophomores	Freshmen
$m = 13.5$	$m = 8.3$	$m = 7.0$	$m = 8.5$
$sd = 2.4$	$sd = 1.5$	$sd = 1.7$	$sd = 1.8$

When to Use the Median

To describe the average of a set of scores, the median should be used only when the mean is inappropriate. The mean is inappropriate for describing a set of scores that is highly skewed. A *skewed distribution* is one in which a minority of participants have scores far above *or* far below the majority of participants. Example 12.7 illustrates what is meant by "a skewed distribution." The distribution in Table 12.D is highly skewed because the vast majority (26 out of 30 of the participants) have scores at the high end (in fact, they are all in the 90s) while a minority (4 out of the 30 of the participants) have very low scores (i.e., scores of 22, 14, 10, and 10).

Example 12.7

A highly skewed distribution:

Thirty high school students in a program for the academically gifted were administered a questionnaire on their attitudes toward higher education. The scores could range from 0 to 100. The distribution of their scores is shown in Table 12.D.

Table 12.D
Distribution of Attitude Scores

Score	Number obtaining each score
100	8
96	7
94	3
93	4
91	3
90	1
22	1
14	1
10	2

The distribution in Table 12.D above has two different averages—the mean (84.8) and the median (95.0). The difference exists because the mean is pulled in the direction of the skew (that is, toward the minority of the scores that lie far below the majority). In Table 12.D above, the minority with low scores (such as the two respondents with a score of 10) has pulled down the mean. Which value is a better representation of the average of this distribution? Statisticians agree almost universally that the median (in this case, 95.0) is more representative of the average in a highly skewed distribution than the mean (in this case, 84.8).

Computing the Median

The median is defined as the average that has half the cases above it and half the cases below it. Example 12.8 illustrates how to compute the median when there is an odd number of ranks.

Example 12.8

Example for computing the median when there is an odd number of scores:

Nine foster child care parents were asked to rate the extent to which their foster children exhibited discipline problems. These are the scores, which form a skewed distribution created by the two very high scores (i.e., scores of 20 and 15):
20, 15, 1, 2, 3, 2, 4, 5, 2

To calculate the median for the data in Example 12.8 above, first put the scores in order from lowest to highest, as shown here:

1, 2, 2, 2, 3, 4, 5, 15, 20

Then count to the middle score. Since there are nine scores, the middle rank is the fifth one (with four ranks above it and four ranks below it). The arrow indicates that the fifth rank up from the bottom is 3. Hence, the median is 3. Put another way, the average respondent had a score of 3.

1, 2, 2, 2, 3, 4, 5, 15, 20
⇧

When there is an even number of scores, count to the middle *two* scores, add them together and divide by two. In Example 12.9, there are eight scores that have been put in order from low to high, with the very high score of 54 creating a skewed distribution. The arrows show the two middle scores.

Example 12.9[3]

Example for computing the median when there is an even number of scores:

3, 4, 5, 5, 6, 7, 7, 54
⇧ ⇧

The median is 5 + 6 = 11/2 = 5.5

Presenting Medians in a Research Report

Like the mean and standard deviation, medians can be presented in a research report in sentences or in tables. Note that the symbol for the median is *mdn*.

When to Use the Interquartile Range

When the median is reported as the average, the interquartile range should be reported as the measure of variability. The *interquartile range* is the range of the middle 50% of the cases.

Computing the Interquartile Range

Example 12.10 shows a set of scores that are highly skewed because of the two very high scores that are distant from the vast majority of the scores. To find the interquartile range for Example 12.10, first put the scores in order from low to high and then divide it into quarters as shown in the example. As you can see, there are four scores below 2.5, four

---

[3] Notice that one of the middle ranks is tied (i.e., the two ranks of 5 are tied with each other). It used to be common to make a slight adjustment in the value of the median using a process called interpolation when there were ties in the middle. Since popular statistical computer programs do not make this adjustment, it has fallen into disuse.

scores between 2.5 and 6.5, four scores between 6.5 and 9.5, and four scores above 9.5. (These are the four quarters.) Thus, the middle 50% lies between 2.5 and 9.5. What is the value of the interquartile range? It is calculated as follows: 9.5 – 2.5 = 7.0. Thus, a researcher can report that the interquartile range is 7.0, which indicates that the middle 50% of the respondents lie within 7 score points of each other.

Example 12.10
Scores divided into quarters to calculate the interquartile range:

1, 1, 1, 2, 3, 4, 5, 6, 7, 8, 8, 9, 10, 11, 120, 150

⇧ ⇧ ⇧

2.5 6.5 9.5

Margins of Error for Means and Medians

For percentages, calculation of the margins of error and the corresponding confidence intervals were illustrated in the previous chapter. The following discussion illustrates how to calculate these statistics for means and medians.

Margins of Error and Confidence Intervals for the Mean

When a researcher draws a random sample from a population and computes its mean as an estimate of the population mean, the estimate may be in error because of random sampling errors. The margin of error for a mean (i.e., the standard error of the mean) is easy to compute as illustrated in Example 12.11.

Example 12.11
Computation of the standard error of the mean:

A random sample of 90 hospital social workers was surveyed with a questionnaire. Among other things, the questionnaire measured their attitudes toward patients with HIV/AIDS on a scale from 0 to 100 (with higher scores indicating more favorable attitudes). The mean attitude score for the sample was 72.5, and the standard deviation was 10.3. To calculate the margin of error, the following formula was used, where s is the standard deviation (i.e., 10.3) and n is the number of respondents (i.e., 90).

$$S_m = \frac{s}{\sqrt{n}} = \frac{10.3}{\sqrt{90}} = \frac{10.3}{9.49} = 1.09$$

The standard error of the mean calculated in Example 12.11 is a *68% margin of error*. Just as with the standard error of a percentage that was considered in the previous chapter, it can be multiplied by 1.96 to get the *95% margin of error*. Thus, 1.09 × 1.96 = 2.1. This indicates that we can be 95% confident that the mean for the population lies within 2.1 points of the sample mean of 72.5.

The researcher who conducted the study in Example 12.11 can now report that the mean attitude score is 72.5, the standard deviation is 10.3, and the 95% margin of error for the mean is 2.1 points.

In addition, the researcher can calculate the 95% confidence interval (95% C.I.) by subtracting the margin of error from the mean (72.5 – 2.1 = 70.4) and by adding the margin of error to the mean (72.5 + 2.1 = 74.6). Thus, the researcher can report that he or she has 95% confidence that the true mean in the population is between 70.4 and 74.6.

Note that the procedure for getting the 95% margin of error for a mean shown above is highly precise only when using samples of about 60 or more participants. For samples with as few as 15 participants, the procedure is only roughly approximate.

Margins of Error and Confidence Intervals for the Median

The computation of the standard error of the median is almost the same as the corresponding calculation for the mean—with the addition of a constant (1.253) as a multiplier in the numerator. This is the formula:

$$S_{median} = \frac{1.253s}{\sqrt{n}}$$

The use and interpretation of the standard error of the median is the same as that for the standard error of the mean. Specifically, the formula immediately above yields the 68% margin of error for the median. Multiplying it by 1.96 yields the 95% margin of error. Subtracting and adding the 95% margin of error from and to the median yields the 95% confidence interval for the mean.

Exercise for Chapter 12

1. Do you anticipate calculating means and standard deviations for your term project? If yes, name the variables for which you will do so.

2. Is it possible that you will be reporting medians and interquartile ranges in your term project? Explain.

3. Do you plan to report margins of error in your term-project research report?

Notes:

Chapter 13

Analysis: Correlation

The most widely used statistic for describing the relationship between two sets of scores is the *Pearson product-moment correlation coefficient*, which is often simply called the *Pearson r* or the Pearson correlation coefficient.[1]

When to Use Pearson *r*

Use the Pearson *r* to describe the direction and strength of a relationship between two sets of scores.

Consider Example 13.1, which shows the scores on an attitude toward technology scale and the scores on an attitude toward the Internet scale. The technology scale has 35 items, while the Internet scale has 10 items. Thus, it is not surprising that the scores on the technology scale are higher than the scores on the Internet scale. However, the researcher is not interested in this artifact produced by the different numbers of items. Instead, the researcher is interested in the relationship between the two sets of scores.

A researcher can determine whether there is a relationship by considering positions of the individuals on the two variables relative to others in the group. Consider Table 13.A in Example 13.1. In it, both Joe and Jane have high scores on attitudes toward technology. (Notice that their scores of 35 and 32 are higher than the scores obtained by others on this scale.) Likewise, Joe and Jane have high scores on attitudes toward the Internet. (Notice that their scores of 9 and 10 are higher than the scores obtained by others on this scale.) At the same time, those who have low attitudes toward technology scores (John and Jake) also have low scores on attitudes toward the Internet. This illustrates what is meant by a *direct relationship* (also called a *positive relationship*). In a direct relationship, high scores on one variable are associated with high scores on the other variable. Likewise, in a direct relationship, low scores on one variable are associated with low scores on the other one.

---

[1] Note that *r* is the symbol selected by Karl Pearson, the statistician who developed the correlation coefficient.

Example 13.1

Table with a direct relationship between two sets of scores:

Table 13.A

A Direct Relationship, r = .89

Respondent	Attitude toward technology	Attitude toward the Internet
Joe	35	9
Jane	32	10
Marilyn	29	8
Phyllis	27	8
Homer	25	7
Clyde	22	8
Jennifer	21	6
Jake	18	4
John	15	5

Notice that the relationship in Example 13.1 is not perfect. For instance, although Joe has a higher technology attitude than Jane, Jane has a higher Internet attitude than Joe. (In other words, while the order on the two variables is similar, it is not exactly the same; hence, the relationship is less than perfect.) If the relationship were perfect, the value of the Pearson *r* would be 1.00. Being less than perfect, its actual value is .89. As you can see in the following number line, which shows the possible values of the Pearson *r*, .89 is a strong direct relationship.

−1.00		Inverse Relationship		0.00		Direct Relationship		+1.00
⇧	⇧	⇧	⇧	⇧	⇧	⇧	⇧	⇧
perfect	strong	moderate	weak	none	weak	moderate	strong	perfect

In an *inverse relationship* (also called a *negative relationship*), those who are high on one variable are low on the other. Such a relationship exists between the two variables in Example 13.2. Those who are high in their fear of animals (such as Robert, Sheldon, and Cynthia) are low in age, while those who are low in their fear of animals are high in age. However, the relationship is not perfect. The value of the Pearson *r* for the relationship in the example is −.85.

Example 13.2

Table with an inverse relationship between two sets of scores:

Table 13.B

An Inverse Relationship, r = −.85

Respondent	Fear of animals score	Age in years
Robert	10	9
Sheldon	8	8
Cynthia	9	7
Nancy	7	12
Elaine	7	13
Turner	6	15
Jackie	4	15
Tom	1	16
Sheila	0	16

The relationships in Examples 13.1 and 13.2 are strong, but in each case, there are exceptions, which make the values of the Pearson *r* less than 1.00 and −1.00. As the number and size of the exceptions increase, the values of the Pearson *r* become closer to 0.00. In fact, a value of 0.00 indicates a complete absence of a relationship. That is, when *r* equals 0.00, there is no discernable trend for the scores on the two variables to put respondents in the same or reverse orders.

Computing the Pearson *r*

The following shows how to calculate a Pearson *r* using a calculator. As you can see, the procedure is complex but manageable. If there is a large number of respondents, a computer program should be used to calculate the Pearson correlation coefficient. (See Appendix D on calculating statistics using free Internet programs.)

For those who want to try calculating the Pearson *r* using a calculator, consider the following example in which attitudes toward illegal drugs will be correlated with respect for authority. To compute the Pearson *r*, first set up a worktable such as that shown in Table 13.C in Example 13.3. Notice that there are two scores per person, and they are listed in columns 2 and 3. To get column 4, simply square the values in column 2 (for example, $5 \times 5 = 25$ for Phil). To get column 5, simply square the values in column 3 (for example, $0 \times 0 = 0$ for Phil). To get column 6, simply multiply the values in column 2 by the values in column 3 (for example, $5 \times 0 = 0$ for Phil). Then sum columns 2 through 6; the sums are shown in the last row of the worktable.

Example 13.3
Example for the computation of the Pearson r:

Table 13.C
Worktable for the Pearson r

Col. 1	Col. 2	Col. 3	Col. 4	Col. 5	Col. 6
Person	Attitude toward drugs	Respect for authority	Col. 2 squared	Col. 3 squared	Col. 2 times Col. 3
Phil	5	0	25	0	0
Bill	7	4	49	16	28
Carol	0	9	0	81	0
Lila	1	7	1	49	7
Frank	4	5	16	25	20
Jackie	2	6	4	36	12
Sum =	19	31	95	207	67

Next, enter the *sums* of the columns in the following formula along with N, which is the number of cases. In this case, there are 6 people responding, so $N = 6$.

$$r = \frac{N(Col.6) - (Col.2)(Col.3)}{\sqrt{[N(Col.4) - (Col.2)^2][N(Col.5) - (Col3)^2]}}$$

$$r = \frac{6(67) - (19)(31)}{\sqrt{[(6)(95) - 19^2][(6)(207) - 31^2]}}$$

$$r = \frac{402 - 589}{\sqrt{[570 - 361][1242 - 961]}}$$

$$r = \frac{-187}{\sqrt{[209][281]}}$$

$$r = \frac{-187}{\sqrt{58729}} = \frac{-187}{242.340} = -.771 = -.77$$

Thus, the Pearson r for the relationship between attitude toward illegal drugs and respect for authority equals –.77. The fact that it is negative indicates that those who have more positive attitudes toward illegal drugs have less respect for authority.

Presenting Values of the Pearson *r* in a Research Report

Like the other statistics in the previous two chapters, values of the Pearson r can be presented in sentences and in tables. Example 13.4 shows three correlation coefficients presented in sentences.

Example 13.4

Correlation coefficients presented in sentences:

There was a strong direct correlation between attitudes toward statistics and attitudes toward math ($r = .72$). In contrast, the correlation between attitudes toward statistics and study skills ($r = .24$) and work habits ($r = .19$) was weak.

The Pearson *r* and the Coefficient of Determination

It is important to note that the Pearson *r* is not a proportion and *cannot* be multiplied by 100 to get a percentage. For instance, a Pearson *r* of .50 does not correspond to 50% of a relationship.

To think about correlation in terms of percentages, values of Pearson *r* must be converted to another statistic, the *coefficient of determination*, whose symbol is r^2, which indicates how to compute it—simply square *r*. Thus, for an *r* of .50, r^2 equals .25 (.50 × .50 = .25). Multiplying .25 by 100% yields 25% as a result. What does this result mean? Simply this: A Pearson *r* of .50 is 25% better than 0.00. Example 13.5 shows selected values of *r*, r^2, and the percentages that should be considered when interpreting values of *r*.

Example 13.5

Values of the Pearson r and the coefficient of determination:

Table 13.D
Selected Values of r and r^2

r	r^2	Percentage better than zero[*]
.90	.81	81%
.50	.25	25%
.25	.06	6%
−.25	.06	6%
−.50	.25	25%
−.90	.81	81%

[*]Also called *percentage of variance accounted for* or *percentage of explained variance*.

Note that it is conventional to give the values of Pearson *r*, but not to report values of r^2 in research reports. However, while discussing the values of *r*, it is helpful to consider how much better than 0.00 they are. For example, a naïve researcher might describe a Pearson *r* of .25 as indicating a moderate correlation. In light of the fact that .25 is only 6% greater than zero (see Table 13.D in Example 13.5), a better interpretation would be that it indicates a weak or relatively weak relationship.

Exercise for Chapter 13

1. Do you plan to calculate values of Pearson r for your term project? If yes, name the pairs of variables that will be correlated.

2. Will you be computing coefficients of determination in order to interpret the values of Pearson r?

Chapter 14

Writing a Survey Research Report

This chapter provides basic guidelines on the preparation of the final report for a term-project survey. Because curriculum objectives vary from course to course, your instructor may require you to make modifications in the material presented below.

The Title

The title should refer to the variables named in the research purpose or hypothesis. For instance, Example 14.1 shows a research purpose with two populations and one variable. Notice that the corresponding title of the research report is very similar to the purpose.

Example 14.1

A research purpose and corresponding title:

Research Purpose: To compare freshman and senior undergraduates' knowledge of the consequences of binge drinking.

Corresponding Title: Undergraduates' Knowledge of the Consequences of Binge Drinking: A Comparison of Freshmen and Seniors

Example 14.2 shows a research purpose with one population and two variables. The subtitle indicates that a survey was conducted, which is optional.[1]

Example 14.2

A research purpose and corresponding title:

Research Purpose: To determine undergraduates' knowledge of HIV transmission and their attitudes toward individuals with HIV.

Corresponding Title: Knowledge of HIV Transmission and Attitudes toward Individuals with HIV: A Survey of Undergraduates

Avoid writing titles that give the results of the research. Because the results of survey research are almost never perfectly clear-cut, indicating results in a brief title is usually an oversimplification of them and can be misleading. See Example 14.3 for a title that inappropriately does this, as well as an improved version of the title.

---

[1] Note that subtitles are not necessary but are often used for the sake of clarity.

Example 14.3

A title indicating the results (not recommended) and an improved version:

Poor title: Men Are More Willing to Drop Off E-waste at Recycling Centers Than Women

Improved Title: Gender Differences in Willingness to Drop Off E-waste at Recycling Centers

The Introduction and Literature Review

The first part of the report should introduce the topic and present the literature review (see Chapter 5 on writing a literature review). For short reports, the introduction and literature review can be integrated into a single essay, with literature cited throughout. In other words, a researcher can use the literature to introduce the topic of the survey. Examples 14.4 and 14.5 show the beginnings of the integrated introductions and literature reviews of two survey research reports.

Example 14.4

Beginning of a survey research report:[2]

Historically, adults with psychiatric disabilities have experienced very low employment rates (11.7% to 30.0%; Rogers, Anthony, Toole, & Brown, 1991; 15%; Anthony & Blanch, 1987). Epidemiological studies of mental illness suggest that low levels of education may be a key factor in low employment rates. Typically, the age of onset of serious mental illness (SMI) occurs in the age range of 17–25 years (Beiser, Erickson, Fleming, & Iacono, 1993; Beratis, Gabriel, & Hoidas, 1994; Blazer, Kessler, McGonagle, & Swartz, 1994; Faraone, Chen, Goldstein, & Tsuang, 1994; Giaconia et al., 1994; Spaner, Bland, & Newman, 1994)—years when many young adults are obtaining higher education and formulating career plans. In today's highly technological society....

Example 14.5

Beginning of a survey research report:[3]

The link between cannabis use and cannabis dependence remains poorly understood. Some researchers contend that cannabis consumption alone will lead to dependence. In a study of U.S. adults, Grant and Pickering (1998) found that risk of cannabis abuse and dependence increased with frequency of consumption. Other work reveals that cannabis consumption alone rarely leads to dependence. Experts liken cannabis's

---

[2] Collins, M. E., & Mowbray, C. T. (2005). Higher education and psychiatric disabilities: National survey of campus disability services. *American Journal of Orthopsychiatry, 75,* 304–315.
[3] Barnwell, S. S., Earleywine, M., & Gordis, E. B. (2005). Alcohol consumption moderates the link between cannabis use and cannabis dependence in an Internet survey. *Psychology of Addictive Behaviors, 19,* 212–216.

addictiveness to caffeine's and conclude that the drug itself leads to dependence less often than many other substances (Franklin, 1990; Hilts, 1994)....

The integrated introduction and literature review should end with a statement of the specific research purposes or hypotheses. For instance, Example 14.6 below shows that the authors of Example 14.4 on the previous page ended their introduction/literature review with a brief summary followed by a statement of the specific research purpose.

Example 14.6

End of the introduction/literature review in a research report [bold added for emphasis]:[4]

In summary, students with psychiatric disabilities are an increasing presence on campuses, and federal policy supports the rights of students with psychiatric disabilities, yet numerous challenges exist for these students. Viewed from either the perspective of mental health advocates or the perspective of higher education administrators, society loses out when the talents of these individuals are under-utilized. **The purpose of this study is** to provide more specific information than has previously been available about the services that exist on college campuses for students with psychiatric disabilities. Study findings can inform state and federal policy and postsecondary institutional practices, with the goal of better serving psychiatrically disabled students to maximize their talents and potential.

The Method Section

The "Method" section, which describes the research methods used to conduct the survey, should immediately follow the introduction and literature review. It should be given a major heading of "Method," which should be in bold and centered on the page. Below this heading should be two subsections: one on participants and one on instruments. These are described below and are illustrated in Example 14.7.

The Participants Subsection

Immediately below the major heading of "Method," the subheading "Participants" should be typed flush left in italics. In this subsection, the sampling procedure should be described in detail, including any restrictions on the sample (e.g., only certain age ranges, only certain occupations, and so on). If random sampling from a population was used, this should be clearly indicated. (See Chapter 6 on sampling.) Describe how potential participants were contacted, how many were contacted, and the percentage that accepted the invitation to participate. Also, if participants were asked to sign an informed consent form, mention the use of the form. See the "Participants" subsection in Example 14.7.

---

[4] Collins, M. E., & Mowbray, C. T. (2005). Higher education and psychiatric disabilities: National survey of campus disability services. *American Journal of Orthopsychiatry, 75*, 304–315.

Demographic information about the sample may be presented in this section. (See Chapter 9 on measuring demographics.) Some researchers prefer to present the demographics at the beginning of the "Results" section, which is described later. Instructors may require that demographic information be placed in one of these two places.

The Instrumentation Subsection

This subsection should immediately follow the "Participants" subsection, and the subheading of "Instrumentation" should be typed flush left in italics.

If existing instruments were used, give the sources (cite and reference them in the same way as literature is cited). Then, summarize what is known about the instruments, with attention to their reliability and validity. (See Chapter 7 on identifying existing instruments and Appendix B for an overview of the concepts of reliability and validity.)

If new instruments were developed for the survey, describe in detail how they were developed. If the instruments were pilot tested (as suggested throughout Chapter 8), indicate how many individuals participated in the pilot test, describe the instructions given to them, and indicate the types of changes that were made to the instruments based on the pilot test. Consider providing examples of the items in the instruments in this section and providing a full copy of the instruments in an appendix to the research report. Example 14.7 illustrates how to describe instrumentation.

Example 14.7

Example of the "Method" section of a research report:

Method

Participants

A simple random sample of 10 class sections of sociology courses was drawn from the master list of all 44 class sections offered at Academia College during the fall 2006 semester. The professors were contacted and asked if they would administer the instruments to their students. Six of the 10 professors (60%) agreed to do so. The 150 students in the six class sections were asked to sign a consent form agreeing to participate. They were assured that their responses would remain anonymous and confidential. All but 2 of the 150 agreed to participate and signed the form, yielding a response rate of 99%.

Demographic questions on the questionnaire revealed that 72.9% of the respondents were undergraduates and 52% were.... [Note that demographics may be reported at the beginning of the "Results" section instead of the "Participants" subsection.]

Instrumentation

The *ABC Attitude Scale* developed by Doe (2004) was used with permission in this study. While Doe did not report information on the validity of the scale, she reported adequate internal consistency (alpha = .88). The scale has been used in two previously published studies (Smith, 2005; Jones, 2006). These authors also reported adequate internal consistency (alpha = .79 and .86, respectively). In addition, Jones reported a high degree of correlation with the previously validated *XYZ Attitude Scale* ($r = .74$), indicating high criterion-related validity.

The *ABC Attitude Scale* contains 20 items regarding methods for teaching the alphabet to preschoolers. For each item, participants responded on a four-point scale from Strongly Agree to Strongly Disagree. Total scores on the scale could range from 0 to 80. Higher scores indicate a more positive attitude toward experience- based learning. A sample item is: "Having much printed material available in the classroom is the best way for children to become exposed to the alphabet." Participants who marked Strongly Agree to this item received four points. Another sample item is: "The best way to teach the alphabet is through practice drills." Participants who marked Strongly Agree to this item received one point. The complete scale (reprinted with permission of Doe, 2005) is shown in Appendix A of this research report.

The Results Section

The results section, which presents the statistics collected in the survey, follows the "Method" section. It should be given a major heading of "Results," which should be in bold and centered on the page.

If the demographics have not been previously described under the "Participants" sub-section, they should be described in this section. Then the results relating to the research purpose and/or hypothesis should be presented.

In the "Results" section, restate the research purpose or hypothesis and then present relevant statistics. If a table is being used to present specific results, summarize the contents of the table and specifically refer to the table as illustrated in Example 14.8. If there was a hypothesis, explicitly state whether the data support the hypothesis, as also illustrated in Example 14.8.

Example 14.8
Example of the "Results" section of a research report:

Results

This survey tested the hypothesis that freshmen would report poorer study habits, less academic self-discipline, and less attention to homework assignments than sophomores. This hypothesis was supported by the averages shown in Table 1, where the means and standard deviations on the three variables are reported. As the data in the table indicate, the average freshman was lower in all three areas than the average sophomore. While the most striking difference was for attention to homework assignments ($m = 7.9$ for freshmen and $m = 12.7$ for sophomores), all three differences are large enough to be worthy of note.

In addition, a purpose of the survey was to explore gender differences on the three variables. Examination of the statistics in Table 2 indicates that women, on average....

The Discussion Section

The "Discussion" section follows the "Results" section. In this section, four matters should be discussed.

First, begin the discussion with a brief review of the research purposes and/or hypotheses and the results relating to them.

Second, describe any implications of the results. (This part of the discussion may be given the subheading "Implications" flush to the left in italics.) The implications should be directly derived from the results. When possible, practical implications should be stated. For instance, if sophomore undergraduates reported much better study skills on average than freshman undergraduates, an implication might be that college administrators pay special attention to diagnosing this and assisting freshmen in improving their study skills.

Third, acknowledge any obvious weaknesses and limitations in the research methodology. (This part of the discussion may be given the subheading "Limitations" flush to the left in italics.) The most common weaknesses are in sampling (such as using biased samples of volunteers) and measurement (such as instruments that are of unknown validity). When weaknesses are serious, readers should be explicitly advised to view the results with caution. Example 14.9 shows how a limitation might be specifically but briefly addressed.

Example 14.9
Description of a limitation in the Discussion section:[5]

Another notable limitation involves Internet-based data collection.... Some individuals with lower education or socioeconomic status may not have access to the Internet, resulting in their exclusion from the study. In addition, although the sample varies demographically in terms of income, education, and state of residence, participants were generally affluent, Caucasian, male, and relatively young. Like many laboratory studies on cannabis... the study sample is largely male. Although analyses revealed no interactions for gender, the preponderance of men in the sample limits the generalizability of findings to women.

Fourth, make suggestions for future research on the topic. (This part of the discussion may be given the subheading "Future Directions for Research" flush to the left in italics.) Example 14.10 shows the recommendations for future surveys made by a team of researchers.

---

[5] Barnwell, S. S., Earleywine, M., & Gordis, E. B. (2005). Alcohol consumption moderates the link between cannabis use and cannabis dependence in an Internet survey. *Psychology of Addictive Behaviors, 19,* 212–216.

Example 14.10

Suggestions for future research in the Discussion section[6]

Future research should examine knowledge of the ADA [Americans with Disabilities Act] with psychometrically sound measures. Insofar as we can determine, the ADA Knowledge Survey represents the first psychometrically sound measure to assess this domain. Disability researchers, rehabilitation psychologists, and others can use this new measure to (a) evaluate the needs of particular segments of the population who are critical to successful ADA implementation, such as business owners, service providers, and employers; (b) evaluate the effectiveness of ADA training and educational efforts; and (c) examine the relationship between ADA knowledge and attitudes toward disability rights and other relevant variables....

Exercise for Chapter 14

1. Write a tentative title for your research report. Present it along with the research purposes or hypotheses to other students for feedback and revise it.

2. Write an introduction for your research report, including the literature review. Present it to other students for feedback and revise it.

3. Write the "Method" section of your research report. Present it to other students for feedback and revise it.

4. Write the "Results" section of your research report. Present it to other students for feedback and revise it.

5. Write the "Discussion" section of your research report. Present it to other students for feedback and revise it.

---

[6] Hernandez, B., Keys, C., & Balcazar, F. (2003). The Americans with Disabilities Act knowledge survey: Strong psychometrics and weak knowledge. *Rehabilitation Psychology, 48*, 93–99.

Notes:

Appendix A
Preparing a Research Proposal

This appendix describes the basics of preparing a written research proposal. While preparing a proposal is an important activity, information on it is presented in an appendix instead of a chapter because a proposal mirrors a final research report in many important respects, and writing a research report is covered in Chapter 14. The relevance of the material in Chapter 14 to proposal writing is described later in this appendix.

Why Prepare a Proposal?

Preparing a research proposal can be helpful for three reasons. First, it can be useful for getting feedback from an instructor on the acceptability of the topic and the research methods that will be employed. Second, a research proposal can be useful for getting feedback from other students, especially those who may have a background and experience in conducting research and analyzing data. Third, a proposal may be necessary when soliciting help in accessing participants. For instance, if a student plans to request permission to administer questionnaires in various professors' classrooms, a written proposal may help the professors understand the nature and purpose of the survey. Finally, many students will need to seek formal permission (from an appropriate administrator or committee) to conduct a survey on campus and the submission of a proposal may be required in order to consider the request. As a prerequisite for this permission, students may have to prepare formal written consent forms for potential participants to sign. The appropriateness of a particular consent form will need to be evaluated in light of the research purposes and procedures, which are described in a research proposal.

When to Prepare a Research Proposal

Work on a written proposal should begin as soon as specific research purposes, questions, or hypotheses have been formulated (see Chapters 1 through 3). Then, as students work through the remaining chapters of this book, they can add material to the proposal.

Elements of a Research Proposal

The elements are described below in the order in which they should be presented in a proposal.

The Title

The first element in a research proposal is a title. There should be a direct correspondence between the title and the research purposes, questions, or hypotheses that will be explored in the survey. See Examples 14.1 and 14.2 in Chapter 14, which illustrate this correspondence.

To distinguish the proposal from the final report, the subtitle "A Research Proposal" may be used in the title of the proposal.

The Introduction/Literature Review

A preliminary introduction/literature review should be the first part of a proposal, beginning just below the title and identifying information on the author (such as the researcher's name, course, and date). See Chapter 4 for information on locating literature on a topic and Chapter 5 for guidelines for writing a literature review.

For short reports on surveys, the literature review serves as the introduction to the research problem. In other words, literature can be cited to introduce the research proposal. It should begin by naming one or more of the major variables in the survey, with information on the variable(s) found in the literature. See Examples 14.4 and 14.5 in Chapter 14 for examples illustrating how a literature review might begin.

The literature review should end with a formal statement of the research purposes, questions, or hypotheses. Example 14.6 in Chapter 14 illustrates how a literature review might end. In the example, it ends with a statement of the purpose of the study.

Since locating and synthesizing literature is a major, time-consuming activity, the first version of the literature review in a research proposal might be a skeleton outline of the available literature and its main thrust. This can then be amplified later in the semester as time permits. Instructors who require the submission of written research proposals may indicate how thorough the literature review should be before its submission.

The Method Section

The "Method" section should be labeled with the word "Method" in bold and centered just below the literature review. It consists of two subsections. The first is a "Participants" subsection, and the second is an "Instrumentation" subsection, each with its own subheadings flush left in italics.

Participants

The first subsection under "Method" is "Participants." This subsection should contain the same types of information as in the "Participants" subsection of a research report (see the information on this subsection on pages 115–116 in Chapter 14, with attention to the first part of Example 14.7 in that chapter). The only difference between the description of participants in the research report and in the proposal is that the material in the proposal will indicate how the researcher plans to solicit participants in the future. Thus, all activities describing the selection of the participants in a proposal should be written in the *future tense*. For instance, a proposal might state that every 10th individual entering the college cafeteria *will be* asked to participate.

Instrumentation

The second subsection under "Method" is "Instrumentation." In this section, begin by describing the instruments that will be used to collect demographic data (see Chapter 9 for information on how to collect such data). If the demographic questions have already been written, they might be presented in an appendix to the proposal.

Then, describe other instruments that will be used. For existing instruments, they should be described in terms of their physical characteristics (such as how many items and the response format, such as multiple-choice). Often, there is published information on the reliability and validity of existing instruments. When it is available, it should be briefly summarized. See the information on this subsection on pages 116–117 in Chapter 14, with attention to the second part of Example 14.7 in that chapter.

For instruments that will be constructed, provide information on what form they might take (e.g., three interview questions on Topic A and four interview questions on Topic B). Including even rough drafts of questions will help in getting feedback on their appropriateness. For new instruments, also indicate whether a pilot study will be conducted to refine them. The use of pilot studies for instrument development is described throughout Chapter 8.

As in the "Participants" subsection, the *future tense* should be used (e.g., "The XYX Scale of Developmental Activities *will be administered* to the parents.")

The Analysis Section

In a research report, this section is called the "Results" section. Because results are not yet available at the time a proposal is written, it is best to call this section the "Analysis" section, with the heading centered and in bold.

This section should indicate how the data will be analyzed for each research purpose, question, and hypothesis. If there is only one of these elements, begin by stating it and then name the statistics that will be computed. If there is more than one research purpose, question, or hypothesis, state each one with a separate statement of which statistics will be computed and reported for each.

As in the "Method" section, the activities in the "Analysis" section should be described in the *future tense*.

The Discussion Section

The "Discussion" section should have a heading of "Discussion" centered and in bold.

As in a research report, this section should begin with a brief review of the research purposes, questions, or hypotheses.

Second, possible implications should be described. This can be done in parallel fashion such as "If the average participant in Group A is found to be *higher* than the average participant in Group B, the implications are.... On the other hand, if the average participant in Group A is found to be *lower* than the average participant in Group B, the implications are...".

Third, the proposal should acknowledge any unavoidable limitations in selecting participants. For instance, if a questionnaire will be mailed, it is reasonable to assume that the response rate will be considerably less than 100%, creating a possible bias. See Example 14.9 in Chapter 14 for a sample statement of limitations regarding sampling.

The proposal should also acknowledge any unavoidable limitations in instrumentation. For instance, a researcher might plan to use self-reports in a survey of marijuana use on campus. Because self-reports are subject to distortion (such as giving socially desirable responses instead of accurate responses), this might be acknowledged as a potential limitation.

The "Discussion" section can be concluded with a statement indicating the importance of the study despite any weaknesses that have been noted. Such a statement might suggest that the study will be worthwhile to undertake despite weaknesses. For instance, it might begin with, "Despite these weaknesses, this study will be the first to provide data on ABS at the XYX campus of the statewide university system. This information will give administrators a basis for determining...."

How Much Detail to Provide

The amount of detail that should be provided in a research proposal will vary from course to course, depending on the curricular objectives and the types of decisions that will need to be made on the basis of the proposal. For maximum feedback on the suitability of proposed research, a proposal should be as detailed as possible.

Concluding Comment

As you can see from the above discussion, there are many parallels between the material in this appendix and the material in Chapter 14. Reading this chapter carefully before writing a proposal should greatly benefit student researchers.

Appendix B

An Overview of Reliability and Validity[*]

For existing instruments used in a term project, students should briefly summarize what is known about the reliability and validity of the instruments in their research proposals (Appendix A) and in their research reports (Chapter 14). This appendix is designed to provide background information for such students.

Reliability and Internal Consistency

The Concept of Reliability in Measurement

Researchers favor instruments that yield consistent scores. In this context, *consistency* is synonymous with the more technical term: *reliability*. A physical example makes clear the need for consistency in measurement. Consider a carpenter who has constructed a doorframe for a new house in an area where the building code specifies that all doorways must be at least 30 inches wide. Suppose further that a building inspector finds that the doorway opening is only 29 inches wide and requires the carpenter to widen it. Then, on the next inspection after it is widened, the inspector declares that it is now only 28 inches wide. These discrepancies indicate a lack of reliability in the measurement of the width of the doorway. The lack of reliability can be attributable to the instrument (perhaps the tape measure is made of rubber) or the person using it (perhaps the inspector is careless in using the tape measure).

Test–Retest Reliability

Test–retest reliability is determined by administering an instrument twice to a sample of examinees. Typically, the two administrations are one or more weeks apart. If a test has good test–retest reliability, those who score high one week will score high the next week when the same instrument is administered to them. Likewise, those who score low one week will score low the next. In even the best instruments, there will be at least some fluctuation from one administration to the next, which will reduce test–retest reliability. This is because of the influence of three factors:

1. Guessing on a test *or* making random marks in response to questions. For instance, some examinees will score higher on one administration of a test than on the other administration due to guessing.

---

[*] This appendix was adapted from: Orcher, L. T. (2005). *Conducting research: Social and behavioral science methods*. Los Angeles: Pyrczak Publishing. Copyright © 2005 by Pyrczak Publishing.

2. Changes in the physical and mental status of the participants. For instance, on the first administration of a test, an examinee might be ill and score lower than on the second administration when he or she feels better.

3. Changes in how the test was administered and for testing conditions. For instance, on one administration of a test, there might be noises that some examinees find distracting that are not present on the second administration.

Reliability is measured with a statistic called a *reliability coefficient*.[1] While it is theoretically possible for reliability coefficients to be negative, in practice they range from 0.00 (indicating no consistency from one administration of the test to the next) to 1.00 (indicating perfect consistency). Tests and scales published by major publishers usually have very high reliabilities, with coefficients typically ranging from 0.85 upward. The consensus among researchers is that tests and scales with reliability coefficients below about 0.70 should be avoided or, if used, the results of the research should be viewed with considerable caution.

In Example 1, the test–retest reliability of the Women's Health Initiative Insomnia Rating Scale is described.

Example 1

A description of test–retest reliability:

Two hundred forty-three women were administered the Insomnia Rating Scale (IRS). The interval between the two administrations varied from 8 days for some of the women to 14 days for others. For the total group of 243 women, the test–retest reliability coefficient was .84. Thus, the IRS scores were acceptably stable over time.[2]

Internal Consistency

Internal consistency (sometimes called *internal consistency reliability*) refers to the consistency of results from one part of a test or scale to another. The meaning of this can be seen by considering an example. Suppose a teacher administered a 40-item history test. For the purposes of studying internal consistency, the teacher scored the odd-numbered items (1, 3, 5, and so on) separately from the even-numbered items (2, 4, 6, and so on). Even though only one test was administered, the teacher now has two scores for each examinee. Correlating the two sets of scores, the teacher can determine the extent to which those who scored high on the odd-numbered items scored high on the even-numbered items, and vice versa. The result of correlating would be called a *split-half reliability coefficient*. Like a *test–retest reliability coefficient*, it has a possible range of 0.00 to 1.00, with 0.70 being the lowest generally acceptable level.

---

[1] Mathematically, a *reliability coefficient* is a *correlation coefficient*.
[2] Loosely based on Levine, D. W., Kripke, D. F., Kaplan, R. M., Lewis, M. A., Naughton, M. J., Bowen, D. J., & Shumaker, S. A. (2003). Reliability and validity of the Women's Health Initiative Insomnia Rating Scale. *Psychological Assessment, 15,* 137–148.

In practice, the split-half technique has been replaced by a more sophisticated form called Cronbach's *alpha* (α). It is mathematically equivalent to splitting a test over and over in as many ways as possible (not just odd- and even-numbered items), computing a coefficient for each possible split, and then averaging the split. Thus, alpha can be defined as a measure of internal consistency based on the average of the coefficients for all possible splits. This is interpreted in the same way as a split-half reliability coefficient, with 0.70 being the lowest generally acceptable level.

What does it mean if an internal consistency coefficient such as alpha is low? It could mean one of two things. First, the scores may have been influenced by guessing or by examinees making random marks. Second, it could be that the scale or test measures more than one skill or trait. For example, consider two mathematics tests for first-graders. The first one contains only one-digit addition and subtraction problems. The second one contains both the one-digit problems and word problems. Other things being equal, one should expect more internal consistency (and a higher alpha) for the first test because its content is more homogeneous. If the test-makers' goal was to measure a homogeneous trait, a low alpha would indicate that the test is deficient in this respect.

Another example will help illustrate why internal consistency is of concern. Consider the Insomnia Rating Scale mentioned in Example 1 above. It is designed to measure a single construct: insomnia symptoms. Because all items are designed to measure this one single construct, there should be high internal consistency. However, if alpha is low, this indicates that the set of items is measuring more than one construct, perhaps because some items were poorly worded, were ambiguous, or did not clearly relate to insomnia. This would call into question the adequacy of the instrument. As it turned out, however, the alpha for the instrument was .79, indicating an adequate degree of internal consistency.[3]

Comparison of Test–Retest and Internal Consistency Methods

Both test–retest and internal consistency techniques provide information that helps in understanding how well a test or scale works. When possible, information on both types should be reported.

Note that test–retest reliability is a measure of consistency across a period of time, while alpha is a measure of consistency among test or scale items at one point in time. Thus, they provide two different types of information. The authors of Example 2 report both types of coefficients. Note that while the values of alpha are at an acceptable level, the test–retest reliability is somewhat low.

---

[3] Loosely based on Levine, D. W., Kripke, D. F., Kaplan, R. M., Lewis, M. A., Naughton, M. J., Bowen, D. J., & Shumaker, S. A. (2003). Reliability and validity of the Women's Health Initiative Insomnia Rating Scale. *Psychological Assessment, 15*, 137–148.

Example 2

A description of internal consistency (alpha) and test–retest reliability:

Internal consistency (coefficient alphas) for the Impression Management subscale scores ranged from .75 to .86 in the previous studies. The test–retest reliability correlation for the Impression Management subscale was found to be .65....[4]

Validity and Its Relationship to Reliability

Validity refers to the extent to which an instrument measures what it is designed to measure. Put in other terms, it refers to the extent to which the scores are *meaningful*.

It is important to note that a test or scale can be highly reliable yet be invalid. For instance, suppose a researcher measures mathematical problem-solving ability with word problems using a test written in English with a group in which some examinees have very limited English language skills. Test–retest reliability might be quite high, with those whose English is very limited scoring low both times. However, for these examinees, the test results would not be a valid measure of mathematical problem-solving ability because the math problems were not presented in a language they could comprehend.

Judgmental Validity

Two types of validity are based almost exclusively on human judgment.

Content Validity

Content validity is based on experts' judgments of the appropriateness of the contents of a scale or test for a particular purpose. For achievement tests, content validity is determined by having experts compare the contents of a test with the instructional objectives contained in a curriculum guide. To the extent that the two are consistent with each other (the test items measure the stated objectives), the test can be said to have content validity.

Content validity can also be used to provide information on the validity of other types of instruments such as personality scales. For instance, the authors of Example 3 validated their measure of emotion regulation for 8- to 12-year-old children using experts' judgments.

Example 3

A description of the content validation of the How I Feel (HIF) scale:

Ten experts in the area of emotional development provided data for the study. Experts were volunteers from among faculty participants in the 2003 Emotional Development Pre-Conference of the Society for Research in Child Development (April, Tampa,

---

[4] Wang, Y.-W., Davidson, M. M., Yakushko, O. F., Savoy, H. B., Tan, J. A., & Bleier, J. K. (2003). The scale of ethnocultural empathy development, validation, and reliability. *Journal of Counseling Psychology, 50*, 221–234.

FL) and included individuals widely known and cited in the area of emotional development. Each expert was provided with a written copy of the HIF. He or she was asked (a) to sort the items into those reflecting positive emotional arousal, negative emotional arousal, and control over positive or negative emotional arousal, and (b) to suggest item additions, deletions, or wording changes.[5]

Face Validity

Face validity is an assessment of validity based on nonexpert judgments of what a test appears to measure on the surface (i.e., on the face of it). For instance, an outsider might examine a nursing test and challenge its validity because it contains math calculation problems. This would indicate that the examination has low face validity. An expert, however, might examine the same test and recognize that the calculation problems are the type nurses use for calculating the dosage of medications to give to patients. Thus, while the *nonexpert's judgment* indicates that the test has low *face validity*, the *expert's judgment* indicates that it has high *content validity*. (See the discussion of content validity above.)

Researchers are mainly concerned with content validity—not face validity. However, face validity becomes a concern if examinees do not think that a test is valid and therefore refuse to take the test or fail to try their best. For instance, applicants to a nursing program might be administered the calculation test described above. Because the items lack face validity for nursing school, the applicants might believe the test is unfair and arbitrary in content.

In short, face validity is more of a public relations concern than a scientific one. Nevertheless, failure of an instrument to have face validity might affect the performance of examinees.

Criterion-Related Validity

Criterion-related validity is based on the extent to which scores on a test or scale correlate with scores on a criterion. A *criterion* is a standard by which something can be judged. For instance, for a new reading test, a criterion might be teachers' judgments of their students' reading abilities. To the extent to which scores on the test correlate with teachers' judgments, the test is said to be valid. Put another way, if one accepts the assumption that teachers are reasonably good judges of students' abilities, a failure of test scores to correlate substantially with teachers' judgments would cast doubt on the validity of the new reading test.

There are two types of criterion-related validity. First, when the instrument is administered at about the same time as the criterion scores are gathered (such as administering a reading test and getting teachers' ratings of students' reading ability at about the same time), the results indicate the instrument's *concurrent validity*.

---

[5] Walden, T. A., Harris, V. S., & Catron, T. F. (2003). How I feel: A self-report measure of emotional arousal and regulation for children. *Psychological Assessment, 15*, 399–412.

The second type of criterion-related validity is *predictive validity*. This is the type of validity that should be determined for all instruments that are designed to predict some future behavior. For instance, algebra readiness tests are designed to measure basic mathematical skills that are needed when learning algebra. The authors of such tests claim that they are of value in predicting the extent to which examinees will be successful in algebra classes. The validity of such a test should be determined by administering it to students who have not taken algebra yet, then collecting a measure of achievement in algebra (such as algebra grades) after they have taken a course, and correlating the results. To the extent that those who score high on the test earned high algebra grades and those who scored low on the test earned low algebra grades, the test can be said to have predictive validity.

Criterion-related validity (both concurrent and predictive) is usually expressed with a *validity coefficient*. Mathematically, it is calculated in the same way as a reliability coefficient. Like reliability coefficients, in practice, they range from 0.00 to 1.00 in criterion-related validity studies.[6] Unfortunately, test makers are typically much less successful in getting high validity coefficients than in getting high reliability coefficients. Although there are no generally accepted standards, these very rough guidelines should be useful to beginning researchers:

Coefficients below .20 = poor validity
Coefficients between .20 and .39 = moderate validity
Coefficients between .40 and .60 = good validity
Coefficients above .61 = excellent validity

Examples 4 and 5 show how concurrent validity was explored in two studies. Note that *r* is the general symbol for correlation coefficients. Because these coefficients are being used to describe validity, they should be called validity coefficients.

Example 4

A description of the concurrent validity of a psychopathy checklist:

Youth Version Scores on the Youth Version of the Psychopathy Checklist correlated with the number of different kinds of criminal activity in which individuals participated ($r = .45$) and the number of different kinds of weapons that adolescents acknowledged using ($r = .37$).[7]

---

[6] Reliability coefficients and validity coefficients are *correlation coefficients*. At this point, note that when a correlation coefficient is used to express the degree of reliability, it is called a *reliability coefficient*. When it is used to express the degree of validity, it is called a *validity coefficient*.

[7] Loosely based on Kosson, D. S., Cyterski, T. D., Steuerwald, B. L., Neumann, C. S., & Walker-Matthews, S. (2002). The reliability and validity of the Psychopathy Checklist Youth Version (PCL:YV) in nonincarcerated adolescent males. *Psychological Assessment, 14*, 97–109.

Example 5

A description of the concurrent validity of an interview measure of gambling behavior:

As part of an interview method for measuring self-reported gambling behavior, gamblers were asked to report the amount of money they spent on gambling over a six-month period. At about the same time, the researchers asked the gamblers' spouses how much they thought was spent on gambling during the same six-month period. These estimates provided by the spouses of gamblers constituted the criterion for judging the validity of the gamblers' self-reports. In other words, to the extent that the gamblers' self-reports correlated with the spouses' estimates, the self-reports would be judged to be valid. The criterion-related validity coefficient was .57, indicating a good degree of concurrent validity.[8]

Example 6 describes a predictive validity study.

Example 6

A description of the predictive validity of the Graduate Record Examination (GRE):

To determine the validity of the GRE General Test for predicting first-year grade point averages (GPAs) in veterinary medical schools, GRE scores were correlated with GPAs earned by students in 16 veterinary medical colleges, resulting in a validity coefficient of .59, indicating adequate predictive validity.[9]

Construct Validity

A *construct* is a label for a cohesive set of related behaviors. For example, "depression" is a construct that is evidenced by behaviors such as inappropriate crying, sleep disturbance, appetite change, and verbalization of suicidal behavior. Researchers cannot directly see depression; they can only see the behaviors that are its indicators. The behaviors that indicate a construct are "cohesive" because they logically belong together.

Construct validity refers to the extent to which an instrument yields scores that are consistent with what is known (or generally believed to be true) about the construct that the instrument is designed to measure. For instance, it is logical to assume that various types of task performance will be hindered by the behaviors that define the construct called "depression." One of the most important types of task performances is job performance in the workplace as indicated by job performance ratings. By correlating scores on a new measure of depression with job performance ratings, information on the validity of the new measure can be obtained. A negative correlation (i.e., those who score higher on depression generally score lower in their job performance ratings) would be expected. If no correlation is found or if a

---

[8] Loosely based on Hodgins, D. C., & Makarchuk, K. M. (2003). Trusting problem gamblers: Reliability and validity of self-reported gambling behavior. *Psychology of Addictive Behaviors, 17*, 244–248.

[9] Loosely based on Powers, D. E. (2004). Validity of Graduate Record Examinations (GRE) general test scores for admissions to colleges of veterinary medicine. *Journal of Applied Psychology, 89*, 208–219.

positive correlation is found (i.e., those who score higher on depression also score higher in their job performance ratings), the results would cast doubt on the validity of the new measure of depression.

Because construct validity can be difficult to understand at first, consider another example. The researchers who were validating the insomnia scale mentioned in Example 1 indicated that it was logical to expect that those who have higher insomnia scores should have lower general health scores. Hence, they correlated participants' insomnia scores with scores on a general health inventory and found a negative correlation, as expected. The correlation, however, was not strong ($r = -.26$), but this was also expected because in addition to insomnia, a very large number of variables impact general health. Therefore, insomnia should not be strongly correlated with general health.[10]

In Example 7, the researchers validated a new measure of the construct called anxiety. Given that it is generally believed that anxiety is debilitating in many ways, they correlated the anxiety scores with scores on a measure of happiness, expecting that more anxious individuals would report being less happy.

Example 7

A description of the construct validity of a new measure of anxiety:

A negative correlation between anxiety and happiness was expected. The Kuwait University Anxiety Scale was administered. To assess self-rated happiness, subjects responded to the statement "I feel happy in general" by marking a number on a scale anchored by 0: No, and 10: Always. Correlations between happiness and anxiety were $-.43$ and $-.44$ for boys and girls, respectively.[11]

Example 8 shows some other relationships that could be examined in order to estimate the construct validity of measures of various constructs.

Example 8

Examples of relationships and differences that could be examined in construct validity studies:

For a new measure of the construct called "social anxiety," positive relationships would be expected between the social anxiety scores and amount of time spent in solitary activities such as recreational reading and playing solitaire.

For a new measure of the construct called "organizational efficiency," organizations that are more profitable should score higher on the average than less profitable organizations.

---

[10] Levine, D. W., Kripke, D. F., Kaplan, R. M., Lewis, M. A., Naughton, M. J., Bowen, D. J., & Shumaker, S. A. (2003). Reliability and validity of the Women's Health Initiative Insomnia Rating Scale. *Psychological Assessment, 15*, 137–148.

[11] Based on Abdel-Khalek, A. M. (2004). Divergent, criterion-related, and discriminant validities for the Kuwait University Anxiety Scale. *Psychological Reports, 94*, 572–576.

For a new measure of the construct called "shyness," students who have high shyness scores should report participating in fewer extracurricular activities.

Distinguishing Between Construct Validity and Criterion-Related Validity

Construct validity provides indirect evidence. For instance, there are many reasons why students might be disinclined to participate in extracurricular activities, with shyness being only one of them (see the last part of the previous example). Contrast this with a criterion-related validity study in which the criterion would be another measure of shyness such as teachers' ratings of students' shyness. Correlating students' self-reports of shyness on the new shyness scale with teachers' ratings of shyness provides much more direct evidence of validity than correlating self-reports of shyness with self-reports of participation in extracurricular activities.

Put another way, in criterion-related validity, two measures of the same construct are used (e.g., self-reports of shyness and teachers' ratings of shyness). In construct validity, the construct (e.g., shyness) is related to a characteristic that should be related (e.g., participation in extracurricular activities).

While criterion-related validity studies provide information that more directly bears on validity, construct validity studies are also highly desirable because they provide a more complex picture of how valid a new measure is. Ideally, both types should be reported for most new measures.

Notes:

Appendix C
Introduction to Statistical Significance

This appendix presents some of the basic concepts underlying statistical significance testing as well as information on when to apply some of the most common tests. Unfortunately, it is beyond the scope of this book to delve into the theory underlying significance testing and the computations of statistics. Students who have no formal training in statistics may not be required to conduct tests as part of their term projects.

Formal significance testing begins with the *null hypothesis*. This is a statistical hypothesis that asserts that any differences observed when studying random samples are the result of random (chance) errors created by random sampling. For instance, suppose a researcher asked a random sample of men in a population and a random sample of women from the same population whether they support legalizing physician-assisted suicide for the terminally ill and found that 51% of the women supported it while only 48% of the men supported it. At first, the researcher might be tempted to report that women are more supportive of this proposition than men. However, the null hypothesis warns that the 3-percentage-point difference between women and men may have resulted solely from sampling errors. In other words, there may be no difference between men and women in the population. Instead, the researcher may have found a difference because he or she administered the questionnaire to only these two particular random samples.

Of course, it is also possible that the men and women in the population are truly different in their opinion on physician-assisted suicide, and the population difference is responsible for the difference between the percentages for the two samples (48% versus 51%). In other words, the samples may accurately reflect the gender difference between the populations. This possibility is called an *alternative hypothesis* (that is, an alternative to the null hypothesis).

Which hypothesis is correct? It turns out that the only way to answer this question is to test the null hypothesis. If the test indicates that the null hypothesis may be rejected, then a researcher will be left with only the alternative hypothesis as an explanation. When a researcher rejects the null hypothesis, he or she has identified a *reliable* difference (i.e., a difference that can be relied on because it probably is not just an artifact of random errors).

Through a set of computational procedures that are beyond the scope of this book, a significance test results in a *probability that the null hypothesis is true*. The symbol for this probability is *p*. By conventional standards, when the probability is as low as or lower than 5 in 100, the null hypothesis is rejected. (Note that a low probability means it is unlikely that the null hypothesis is true. If something is *unlikely* to be true, it is rejected.)

The formal term researchers use when discussing the rejection of the null hypothesis is *statistical significance*. For instance, the following two statements might appear in a research report:

The difference between the means of the liberals and conservatives is statistically significant ($p < .05$).

The difference between the means for the men and women is *not* statistically significant ($p > .05$).

The first statement says that the probability that the null hypothesis is true is less than ($<$) 5 in 100; thus, the null hypothesis is rejected and the difference is declared to be statistically significant. The second statement says that the probability that the null hypothesis is true is greater than ($>$) 5 in 100; thus, the null hypothesis is *not* rejected, and the difference is *not statistically significant.*

In other words, significance tests help make decisions based on the odds that something is true. All individuals do this in everyday life. For instance, when an individual prepares to cross a busy street, he or she looks at oncoming vehicles to judge their speed and distance to see if it is safe to cross. If such an individual decides that there is a *low probability* that it is possible to cross the street safely, he or she *rejects* the hypothesis that it is safe to cross the street.

In Table C.1 are the names of some of the most popular basic significance tests and when they can be used. Keep in mind that all significance tests result in a probability of the truth of the null hypothesis, and the probability values are interpreted as indicated above.

Table C.1

Popular Basic Significance Tests

Name of test	Purpose
z test and t test	To compare two means; to compare two Pearson correlation coefficients.
Analysis of variance (ANOVA)	To compare two or more means.
Mann-Whitney U test	To compare two medians.[1]
Chi-square test	To compare two or more percentages.[2]

[1] Technically, this is a test of distributions. If the distributions are significantly different, it is safe to assume that the medians are significantly different.
[2] Chi-square calculations are performed on frequencies, but the results apply to the percentages derived from the frequencies.

Appendix D

Free Internet Programs to Calculate Statistics

In statistics courses, students are often taught how to use commercial software programs, such as SPSS, to calculate statistics. These programs typically are very powerful, permitting complex analyses of large amounts of data. Students who have learned how to use one of these programs will probably want to use it in the analysis of their term-project data.

While commercial programs have the advantage of being able to perform complex analyses on large amounts of data, they may have the disadvantage of being difficult to learn. Fortunately, a number of free programs on the Internet are easy to learn and can be used to calculate the limited number of statistics mentioned in this book. The following are two that are relevant for the analysis of term-project survey data.

http://home.ubalt.edu/ntsbarsh/Business-stat/otherapplets/Descriptive.htm

This interactive Web site permits entry of scores on one variable for one population. After the scores have been entered, clicking on "Calculate" yields a number of statistics, including the following statistics that are mentioned in this book:

- mean
- standard deviation
- median
- interquartile range (identified as "InterQuartile")

http://faculty.vassar.edu/lowry/corr_stats.html

This interactive Web site permits entry of scores on two variables for one population. After the scores have been entered, clicking on "Calculate" yields a number of statistics, including the following statistics that are mentioned in this book:

- mean
- standard deviation (identified as "Std.Dev.")
- standard error of the mean (identified as "Std.Err.")
- Pearson r

Keep in mind that Web sites sometimes change their content, change their addresses, and sometimes cease to exist without notice. If this is the case when accessing any of the above sites, go to **www.StatPages.net**, which, at the time of this writing, provides links to 380 interactive Web sites that perform calculations. Additional ones may also be found by using a search engine such as Google with search terms such as "statistics calculate program."

Notes:

Notes: